PAIN

Abuse Doesn't Discriminate

Julia Greaves

Pain

ISBN: 978-1-7385728-0-9

First published in Great Britain in 2024 through
Amazon self-publishing service

Produced by samanthahoughton.co.uk

Contents

Acknowledgments

My family are my world and, at times, the only reason I survived this ordeal. I thank you for putting up with me, especially my Mum. Writing this has helped me understand what a huge part she has played in my and my children's/ grandchildren's lives. Your calmness, which has sometimes driven me beyond despair, was your way of coping. It cannot have been easy.

Also, this is in memory of my grandad, who, in times of despair, I look up to the stars and curse you, asking where you are. I also get bit in the arse by the insects when I am chatting to you tidying up the grave.

And now to my Dad, who was fully aware that I was writing this book but never made it to read or see it published. I hope you are proud now, Dad, and I know you would have asked some questions or made up a silly song.

I also want to thank DB, my good friend Lucia, for helping me with the grammar with the early edits and VP and AP with helping me with the website. Also Samantha Houghton for her help and support with my book, Amal Instagram @mve. and Mr. & Mrs. John, thank you for encouraging me never to give up on my dreams.

Introduction

I started writing this book in 2013. I had been to see a consultant who informed me that I needed surgery, which could leave me in a wheelchair if the surgery went wrong. I would have five years of relatively normal life if it were successful. At forty-five years of age, a degenerative condition I was born with destined me to have an operation designed for older people. Or did the many years subjected to domestic abuse play a part?

I believed I had finished the book in 2020, and it was ready to be published; however, as you continue to read, my life turned completely around at the beginning of 2022, after a lifetime of a cyclone of destruction and pain. You know, life turns on us for a reason. It was not the right time, and there was an additional chapter to add. Never ever take life for granted, never stop trusting and loving, but always learn that often it's not you, it's them.

I am dedicating my story to people out there experiencing all kinds of abuse, especially during and after the many Covid lockdowns. Statistics state that the lockdowns will produce generations of casualties, both victims and perpetrators of abuse. I hope this will provide an understanding of how and why people behave in such a manner. Abuse is like COVID-19; it doesn't discriminate.

I want to, therefore, pass my love and strength to all of you who are suffering. All of you may not get through it, but please try and understand that it was not your fault - sometimes it's the required healing and not so much the blame.

I've based the characters in this book on real people, but I have changed their names. I will go back to my childhood and debunk the myth that abuse comes from poverty and deprivation. As I said before, abuse does not discriminate. Still, one can often find it hidden in the high class, middle class, working class and people known as the "underclass", labelled as some subordinate intergenerational class. It's not just people experiencing poverty and hardship. Many are perceived to have everything, but underneath the designer clothes, cars, and beautiful houses, they are chasing demons or having demons chase them. It's easier to hide; it may appear as an awkward whisper or in an inappropriate tweet.

Some people in desperate times have demonstrated complete kindness when they have nothing but wisdom and experience to offer. Their lack of education and years of being told they are nothing grounded them down to the lowest of the low. I have supported many at work or in my friendship groups; in domestic abuse situations, the ideology to raise their self-respect and self-awareness which helps them confidently move on and identify it is not their fault. A survivor of domestic abuse will undoubtedly show perpetrator traits. There will be behaviours picked up by the survivor that mirror the perpetrator. Sometimes, the survivor becomes the perpetrator but remains the survivor in the relationship. Some books and programmes identify a perpetrator's behaviour despite the opinions of others who state, "I would never let that happen to me".

I am a survivor of abuse, but at times, I displayed my weaknesses by hurting others when I should have "turned the other cheek and walked away with my head held high". I often wonder if other survivors are embarrassed and ashamed. Or is this ignorance? I never trusted anyone apart from family members or my best friends. I held all men in the same contempt as the ones who abused me, except one whom I fell in love with to start a new journey.

A mother's love for her children should be unconditional, but there are times when anyone can interpret the blindness of abuse as weakness or slutty behaviour. As a parent, there are times when we cannot determine why our children are behaving in such a manner; why couldn't we work out what was happening to our children? Why weren't we warned?

It's very difficult to balance a relationship, especially when children come along. The privacy and time spent together often just get blown out the window, and the formidable demands of a child come in. When someone is so intensely jealous, it is often difficult to decide to neglect your needs for the sake of your child. Your partner will often make unreasonable demands of time, attention, household chores, and sex. They want you all to themselves. How many times can you resonate with the expectancy of Sunday morning sex - when the door is locked, and you can hear the children calling for you? But then you get moaned at as you appear not to be enjoying the lovemaking! Or your friends come to visit, and the partner often sabotages the conversation or bangs cupboards and doors. So often, the abuse will often impact the children without the parent or guardian ever realising it. "Oh, it's just them, they are tired" or "no they really like you". "No, it's my fault; I should be spending time with them," and so on.

When you reflect on the abuse, it will raise an awful, guilt-ridden, gut-wrenching anger as you ask yourself why you didn't walk away earlier. As a child, I had a relatively normal childhood with parents who loved me, so why did I accept this disgusting treatment and ignore the red flags? But as you will realise as you read, from an early age, I had forgotten about the various incidents that had occurred. Instead, I believed I deserved this and must get on with it, or it would get better, and he loved me so much! The kids needed their dad around; what did people think? Who would have me? Who would want me? What is a normal relationship when so many couples are together and come across as so happy? What was wrong with me? I concluded that it must be me. I deserved this treatment.

I come from a decent 2:2 (statistically correct) family; both my parents worked hard and were together until the sad death of my father in 2022. We were a unit, had a safe home, and everything we wanted as children, but they were unable to protect me from hidden vulnerabilities as a child. My family labelled me slightly eccentric, mischievous, mad, and strong ("just like your grandmother"), but I am not sure they ever understood me except my mum. It is not enough for a parent to provide a child's basic needs. I was never starved or beaten; financially, they gave me what they could afford, and we had a nice house. I was accepted for being

Julia by my loving grandad and entertained my family with my eccentricity and weirdness.

To my family and friends, thank you so much for supporting me with this book. It will be a little uncomfortable to read at times. You may not be aware of everything that's gone on, but I love you all and thank you again.

1 | Football

I have been vulnerable since I was a toddler. I was the child who found the paint in the shed and then was found covered in it - doing my own thing! I was the child who used to cut dollies' hair, pull out eyes, and undress them. I was the child obsessed with drawing bodies and beautiful pictures of the perfect girl. I had an awful temper but a charming personality. I would smile at people when I was being naughty, described as that cheeky, cute little girl. Now, I probably would be labelled with a disorder and have intensive therapy. But then, I was described as 'slightly odd' and accepted by my family.

When I was little and refused to go to bed, Jack Frost would come and nibble my toes. I swear I saw this image of a boy with a striped jumper and stone eyes looking at me when it was frosty. I wet the bed until I was seven; my Mum would patiently change the bedclothes and not tell me off for doing it.

I never felt good enough, I was accepted, but Dad had always been the type to take the piss out of me rather than encourage or show his love. As a child, I never went hungry.

I always had lots of clothes and toys, but emotionally, my Dad never really understood my sensitivity.

My brother, however, was the child who was quite compliant and good at sport. My Dad was obsessed with sports, particularly football, so sometimes, my brother was pressured to be the best. This was very frustrating for him. I wasn't as sneaky, so I would get caught when retaliating. Because he was so much stronger than me, I used ammunition and planned my attacks on him. We used to play boxing matches; I had boxing gloves, and he used his bare fists. I was brought up on a street with boys and surrounded by boys at weekends for football. My brother was not a natural mixer; he used to stand on the edge of what was happening where I was in the middle. He always dragged me out of trouble or ran to Mum.

When I used to throw knives at him or hit him in the stomach with my huge paint set, I got my legs slapped and told off by my Dad as it would stop him from playing football. The back of my legs were often slapped by Mum. I probably deserved it and would get another for not showing remorse.

From as young as I could remember, I spent Saturday and Sunday wintry mornings watching my older brother, Liam, play football on a freezing football field. I used to make a fuss about wanting to watch SWAP Shop, but no, I had to go as the topic of sport overwhelmed anything else in our household. My Dad usually bribed me with a bag of sweets. We'd spend time in a pub garden following the match, or we made do in the town centre and went to the Carnival pub. The Carnival pub was built bang in the middle of the town, and around it was a plot of large rocks with a huge waterfall. (The council took it down sometime later due to health and safety issues). No one cared in the 1970s - there was a high number of children who had split their heads and broken limbs crossing those rocks. It was rough, with no supervision, and we would run through the lower and higher levels playing run-outs. It was good in the summer, and if there were plenty of kids about, but just Liam and me during the winter, was cold and boring. We would sit in the lobby and have the usual bottle of Coke and KP crisps, but that was boring, too. Nobody thought of paedophiles or the risk of someone grooming you to have sex. Grown-ups told us not to speak to strangers or, if a dirty old man approached us, run home or go into the pub.

One Sunday morning, there were a lot of boys playing football outside The Carnival pub; I was bored. There are only so many times you can play on the rocks. Suddenly, I felt a pain in my neck, and my head went straight back. Someone found kicking a ball at my head funny while I was drinking my Coke. The glass bottle caught my lip, causing it to bleed and chip my tooth. The parents of the lad continued to drink inside. Despite the boys laughing, everyone deemed it as an accident. I was the only girl - so who would back me up?

This was one of many times when I felt alone and like one of the boys, although I was the only girl. I was known as little Liam's sister. Liam was a very talented footballer, good at athletics and everything except swimming. Incidentally, I was good at swimming while that shivery skinny boy hated it. I don't remember going that much, though. Our parents really focused on Liam's football; although they took me to ballet and dancing classes - a pink flowery tutu didn't get me excited as I was so used to playing with the boys. I loved that I could go out in the streets so much that I ran out into the street at age four without any knickers! Of course, they all laughed at me.

I didn't like football despite it being the main theme in my house. I was into clothes (just not ballet tutus), fashion and dressing up dolls - making them look ugly and pretty. The tomboy part of me used to play run out in the streets and fool the Asian shopkeeper with my sweetness while I nicked the sweets. So maybe I was born with this spirit, as my Mum would never have encouraged me to steal, but she never knew. She said I never liked men from being a baby, only my Grandad and Uncle Jeremy. I did not even like my Dad. And yet I grew up in a street with only boys, and I have many years of experience with football teams, soccer presentations and football jumble sales. I wanted to shriek, "Get me out of here!" But there are times as children when we do not understand our parents' lives and what they are going through. My Mum tried her best; I couldn't ask for a better Mum and Nan for my children and grandchildren. She has the strength of a lion and the wisdom to say her favourite line, "put it down to experience." She doesn't judge; she is there. Amazing woman.

Feeling hard done by and not fitting in, my escape was my grandparents - their home was my sanctuary - I often asked if I could stay. I was an angry child, but as soon as I walked through that door, I became the apple of my Grandad's eye. They lived on a council estate in Tottenham. It was a two-bedroom house with no central heating, one bathroom, a tiny kitchen, a back room and a front room. It had a tiny backyard and a front garden. Everyone's house looked the same; they all had similar council wallpaper from a choice of five designs, so it was highly unlikely any of the houses were unique.

My Nan had the biggest clothes collection for a lady of that time. She loved her clothes, new, designer, second hand; she wanted them all. My Nan had been ill all her life, very sickly, but don't underestimate this woman. As others told me, her name was 'Acid Agnes', as she was direct and never had any compassion for people's feelings. I was the daughter she never had. She was a spiritual lady, and most nights, she would tell me about parties in the war and how she would contact the dead through mediums. She had the gift of seeing things. Every night, I would ask her to go through our family album, dating back to the 1800's. I knew every family member; their sense of dress was immaculate. We would go through the photos and pics, looking at the outfits and then scaring me half to death by telling me that the bed I was sleeping in was where her father had died. The room was cold and dark; the huge oak wardrobes and shadows scared me but were also comforting. My Nan had the sharpest tongue and cheekbones and a defined face when she was younger. None of the family noted her looks, but I never heard her compliment these attributes. She was Agnes; others knew her as weird and troubled, but I got her.

My grandad was eight years older than my Nan; he was handsome and smart. He called me toffee nose, and I was his toffee, as I always had food around my mouth and up my nose. He also called me Kipper, as I never shut up and would talk to him for hours and hours. This man had served in the war but never spoke about it. Only twice did I hear him badmouth someone. He couldn't bear liars and thieves, yet he was a bookies' runner and drank a lot after the war. He wasn't a very attentive father to my Dad; he was always settling bets at the pub. But they had money; my Nan had mink coats, all the top-of-the-range clothes, amongst the council wallpaper. Funny that!

Every Saturday, Nan and I would go down to Wood Green shopping Centre, and we would both get an outfit of our own choice. Once a year, we would go to Selfridges to buy a new coat, new outfit, and shoes. We would also watch a pantomime and eat in a restaurant. Liam used to dread this day, as he hated trying on clothes. I loved it at my Nan's - there was no making me eat at the table; I could eat what I wanted, do what I wanted, without any restrictions involving football. They took me to ballroom competitions, and we used to look at all the makeup and dresses. I was in my element. My uncle even promised for me to have training, but then it all stopped.

I remember sticking my head out of the window, watching who was walking about and the smell of the roses in the front garden. Neighbours were in the garden pruning bushes. It was all so peaceful, and the sun always seemed to shine. There was an Irish family at the end of the street - a house full of kids and adults. They were often drinking, smoking and eating fry-ups. Nan kept me from mixing with too many people. There was another family a couple of doors down; she was a quiet woman living with her daughter. Nan's friend Bea would often pop in for a chat, and she started to bring her daughter Megan.

I hated Sundays as I knew I would have to go back home and to school the next day. I loved the school holidays so I could get away from the pubs, football, boys, the attention on how great my brother was, and feeling useless. It is just something to take note of when siblings fight. It can become a learned behaviour pattern for the weaker and more vulnerable.

2 | Megan

Nan's friend's daughter, Megan was about fourteen years old, and I was seven when she started to visit with her mum. Nan said she was going to a catholic school but got chucked out, so she wasn't at school each day. Megan was a large, freckly girl who always wore a denim jacket and clogs on her feet. I used to think that was a funny combination, and she had a short haircut that looked like a monk. Bea said that Megan liked me and it was where she could be kept an eye on. To this day, I do not know why the school expelled her or what she had done. Grandad didn't talk much to Bea and said nothing about Megan. Nan kept saying she was fat and questioned how anyone could let their daughter get like that, but she enjoyed Bea's company.

There were two rooms downstairs at my Nan and Grandad's; we had the posh front room and the back room. The back room everyone used, saving the front room only for guests. The cupboards were full of ornaments; doilies were on the chairs, and fake flowers were in vases. And an old gramophone in the corner. This was the main room where I read, and I used to read a lot of Enid Blyton. I loved the

Enchanted Wood and the Faraway Tree. They were about magical characters that lived in a tree that came to life.

I existed in a land that never forgot at the top of the tree, and there was nothing about football. It was my fantasy; I wanted to be part of a bright, vibrant life with beautiful dresses and clothes and people who were odd but accepted. I was part of that tree ... I was that little girl with a good imagination writing poems and stories for my Nan to read. Except I didn't show her everything.

I often sat in the back room with Nan and Grandad, drawing, making dresses, playing with my two dolls and listening to Bea. Megan wasn't always there at the beginning, and she kind of frightened me, but then she started to come into the house. Megan was very surly, and I'd see her bloated, freckled face as she sat in the corner. Once, Megan asked if I wanted to go into the front room as she couldn't hear properly and wanted to see what I was doing. I asked Nan, and she said yes. I wasn't sure where my Grandad was, but it was harmless. We sat on the sofa and just chatted. Then Megan went home with Bea. I was there a lot during the holidays and weekends. Megan sometimes would come with Bea and ask if we could go into the front room. Sometimes, Nan said yes, while Bea said they would say no as they were not stopping long.

Megan asked if we could go to the old Rec Park one day. Now, this park was fabulous, and they had free bikes you could hire. Liam and I used to go on a Sunday afternoon, but Nan would not let me go by myself as she said some weirdos that hang around there might take me away. I loved that park; Nan told me about an air raid shelter blown up during the war, which left many bodies scattered around the park. It never worried me; death was part of living; remember, Nan often spoke about spirits and ghosts. It was the living that would eventually try and destroy me. So, we went to the park.

Often, I would go to the hairdressers and watch Nan and Bea get their weekly set, and then we'd go back home. Grandad would be having a kip as he used to work as a pot man at weekends and was often down the betting shop, too.

It was a Saturday, and Megan knocked on the door. She did not want to go to the park on that occasion; I'm not sure why, but it may have been raining that day. She asked where Nan and Grandad were. Grandad was upstairs, and Nan was out. We went into the front room and sat down. She was wearing her usual denim jacket, clogs and big white socks. She had large white thighs. I brought my books in, and she asked me about their characters. I said they were Moon Face and Silky the Fairy. With that, she put my hand on her thigh and asked if it felt silky. I said no that it felt hairy and to get off of me. She then asked if I had ever seen a Mary Hairy. I explained that I had never seen one. Did she mean holy Mary? I knew she was a Catholic. I did not associate the word vagina with fanny; Mum used to call it a lily, so if anyone was called Lily, I found it amusing.

She opened her legs and said, "Don't you ever tell your Nan what I am going to do."

Nan had a little footstool, a prized possession family heirloom; Megan picked up the stool and placed it in front of me; how she got on it, I don't know; her arse must have been hanging off it. Megan took off her knickers.

"What are you showing me?" I asked.

She said, "This", and to my horror, she opened her legs to reveal her hairy patch.

It was curly and auburn, and I gasped.

"That's a hairy Mary. Do you want to touch it?"

Of course, I never; the thing was bloody frightening to a seven-year-old, but part of me was excited and curious. Why was mine smooth and small? I didn't have any hair. We were both girls. I had never examined my lily before; it was something you had a wee from. She then said to tell nobody.

Of course, I later asked Nan why I didn't have hair around my lily, and she said I would when I got older. But if I washed my three f's (face, feet and fanny), I had nothing to worry about.

It was a few weeks before Megan came to see me; she had been caught shoplifting, so she was grounded.

We went into the front room again, and she told me to shut my eyes, which I did. She said, "Pretend you are Silky, and I am Moon Face. I am big, and you are a little fairy."

She then sat me down and kissed me on the lips.

"I like you, Silky."

She touched my face and stroked my shoulders, over my flat little bumps and under my polo neck. I couldn't ask what she was doing as she kept kissing me. She then put her hand inside my trousers and into my knickers, touching lily. I responded by trying to move my face, but she kept rubbing her hand on my lily. The touching didn't feel bad, but the rubbing made me uncomfortable. Once again, she said not to tell anybody, or she'd take my books so I couldn't read them.

I asked Nan to ensure she kept my books in my room or the back room, as I did not want Megan to see them. Nan did not ask why; Grandad said something wasn't right about that girl, and why wasn't she going to school? She was also too old to be playing with a seven-year-old.

Nan said, "It keeps her out of trouble. Bea said she can keep an eye on her."

So, the next time, that fat, disgusting girl opened her legs again and made me stroke her hair; it didn't feel nice; it felt coarse, and she smelt sweaty. She seemed to go red and sweaty when I touched it. She then sat on the stool, opened her legs and showed me what was underneath her hair. It looked like a snail that somebody had stamped on.

"What's wrong with it," I asked.

She then told me to come over to the stool, and she put her hands down my trousers, under my knickers, gently stroking lily. It wasn't rough like the first time; it felt nice. I did want to go for a wee, though, so I returned to the front room after going to the toilet. She told me to touch the snail and feel how slimy it was. I was a curious child, so I did. She was red by now; she asked me to stroke it like I stroked my doll's hair. She shut her eyes. I looked at that ugly, freckled, fat red face, but after a few times, I became bored. It was making my fingers sticky and smelly. It was a smell like I had never experienced. My lily never smelt like that!

This happened about three times, not all at once, but on three separate visits; I said my fingers smelt, and I didn't like it. She said it was fine and wouldn't do it to me but to watch what she was about to do. She opened her legs, showing me her disgusting, battered, hairy beaver. Oh no, I wanted to go to the park, not watch that! She started to stroke herself and breathe heavily. Then she opened those fat thighs even more and stuck her finger inside, but not inside the wee hole; there was another hole. I was confused; I knew it wasn't her bum. Thank God she didn't subject me to that; her hairy Mary had been enough. She started quickly shoving her finger in and out of this hole. The noise and the smell were unbearable, so I ran out of the room. I went straight to the toilet and had a wee, but I couldn't find the other hole when I examined myself. She must have made that hole herself.

Then I went into the room next door. By then, Grandad had come downstairs and asked if I was okay. I said to him that Megan smelled. He laughed at me and said I didn't have to play with her if I didn't want to. So, what she did must be okay! She definitely smells, though.

Megan left me alone for a few weeks and never suggested going into the front room. I started writing about Moon Face kissing Silky in my notepad, smelly Mary, and dirty fingers. When Megan next came to visit, she made me touch her tits: she had enormous saggy tits, she never smelt nice, and they never felt nice. She would again ask me to touch her hair and then her boobs. She asked me to slide my fingers inside her snail; it looked like Brian, the character from the Magic Roundabout. I liked the magic roundabout; I saw nothing wrong with the snail. It got smellier and smellier; it began to dribble down my little fingers, and I didn't like it.

So, I stopped, and she said, "I'll tell your Nan and Grandad."

I replied, "They know, and my Grandad said I don't have to play with you. I don't like this game."

I did not have to touch her again for the next couple of weeks, but she would send notes to Silky from Moon

Face about waiting for a kiss and cuddle. I was quite happy reading notes; some things I didn't quite understand, but I still read them. I heard the word 'fuck', but that was when an adult was angry.

Megan's tactics had begun to change. She knew when Grandad went to bed and Nan was around the hairdressers, meaning we were alone downstairs. She made me read the notes, and then, under a pillow, she would take her knickers off and ask me to lie on top of her. I was fully clothed, never naked, and she couldn't touch me with those stinky hands. She would try to kiss me. She smoked fags; I could smell them, and her breath smelt.

The last time Megan touched me before Nan found out, she came in with her bloated, sweaty, freckled face; I can remember her smell to this day. Grandad knew I wanted to draw and play with my dolls and told Megan I wasn't well. I hid the notes Megan wrote in the small vases on the mantlepiece. Nan found the notes the next day and asked who'd written them; I said, Megan. I assumed they knew she had been showing me her snail, and I told Nan she didn't wash, how she smelled and how she told me not to tell her. Nan took the notes and went straight round to Bea's.

I never saw Bea or Megan come into Nan's again. Bea sent Megan away to live with her aunt, and then Bea exchanged her home for another house from the council. They both moved away, and no one ever mentioned it again.

3 | School Years

My first memory of school was at a London nursery. It was a very old Victorian school, which appeared huge to a little four-year-old. I remember the big dapple-grey rocking horse I constantly wanted to ride, and the smell of school dinners wafted through the perimeter as Mum walked me into the school, and that smell never left me. My first primary teacher used to pick me out in class, and according to my mum, she did not like her little girl. I did not get very good reports on parents' evenings, and the school often called Mum in. Why? Because I had spirit! The infant's school really concentrated on reading and writing skills. Every Sunday night at our little house in Edmonton, Mum would give us our spelling tests and times table. Mum knew I hated Maths but encouraged me with my writing and spelling. She would also call out tables as we walked to school, so I felt like a scholar by the age of six.

We moved when I was around eight or nine. I felt sad leaving the area and leaving my friends, but we really needed a bigger house. The next school had an old deputy head we named "Squizzie"- she was a vicious old trout using the slipper to reprimand anyone. She wore her hair in a bun, and I remember her glasses hung off her long, thin nose. We were all terrified of her. The head teacher was a kind, large man, but he died just as the school had enrolled me. At the memorial assembly, pupils and teachers cried throughout the service, and I looked around at everyone crying, feeling sadness.

Once again, teachers called my Mum and Dad into the school as we were writing a composition, and I had written about a rapist. It contained nothing sexual but physical violence - biting chunks out of little kid's arms and legs, following them and scaring them. Mum just explained that I had a vivid imagination, not knowing this could have been from the days in Nan's front room with Megan!

I smoked at an early age and sucked my thumb until ten years old. This made my teeth stick out. Mum would take me on two buses to the private orthodontist every few weeks. But then I used to eat toffee to remove the brace, to try and dislodge it, as I felt even uglier. Once again, she was trying to help, but boy, I gave her a hard time on every journey. I now have straight teeth and have never had a filling. I felt she never cared about me, but I was a strong, determined young person full of anger and bitterness towards her. My Dad encouraged this.

I was sure they were going through a wobbly patch then, and his leniency towards me was aimed at her. Mum said that the atmosphere in the home changed as soon as I walked through the door. I can honestly say that I wanted everyone to be as miserable as me. I would start on anything, a parking space or my clothes not ready to wear. Mum used to iron my clothes, and I would throw them on the floor. I would call my Mum awful names, and Dad would sit there; that's when he wasn't down the pub. We would fight and shout at each other. It was the come down from the drugs and probably the lack of energy and motivation from not eating. I bathed, changed clothes and got the fuck away from them.

I did not go to the same school as my brother. I disliked the rules and regulations of the school, so I was not enthusiastic about going. He used to get a bus to school, whereas I could walk around the corner to mine. From the day I entered that school, a boy used to wait at the top of the road to walk with me. I also used to walk and knock on my friends Suzy's door and then get our fags at the local corner shop. My parents knew that I smoked; what they did not know was that I spent the dinner money they gave to me in that shop. I used to get hungry, but the lure of smoking in the bathrooms gave me that assurance of being part of a group.

I scored A and A plus despite my reluctance to attend school - I was on my way to success until about thirteen years when I started to bunk off school, and eventually, at fourteen, I left to work in a clothes shop to earn money. I used to go back for odd periods, which I enjoyed but generally didn't want to take part in PE where the girl's bodies would be different to mine. They were sprouting breasts and talking about getting off with boys. I felt out of place, so my education suffered. I wrote fake notes and copied my parents' signature. Little did I know that my mum telephoned the school every day to see if I was in school. I went in sometimes, then walked blatantly out of the gate. Dad would often take me to work and give excuses to Mum, who was tearing her hair out with me. She saw such potential in me but could not get through to him why it was so crucial for me to go to school. In lessons, particularly Math's, I refused to take a pen or write anything down and threw a chair at a teacher when she would not allow me to go to the toilet. So it was easier for me to do my own thing.

I went to work, and the school agreed for me to attend the examinations and then leave. Years later, the boy who waited for me at the corner asked if I had left to go to another school. He persisted for many years, waiting at the top of the road, frightened to come and knock on my door. Only a couple of years ago, he told me he'd had a massive crush on me, which lasted many years. Knowing this many years later, I was absolutely flabbergasted; who would fancy me at that age? I was riddled with Anorexia by that stage and would always wear baggy clothes to try and avoid showing my flat chest and curve-less body. It did not occur to me that he liked me for being me. I joined in throwing eggs and flour on the last day of school before finally leaving, and then during our last walk home, I said, "thank god I never have to do this again".

I have apologised to him since, and we regularly meet up. We have a group on Facebook, and a few photos of me are there. He is still a chatterbox but kind; he is a very special person in my life, and I can tell him anything. We share the same birthdays, too. He also still likes me for being me.

At the age of fourteen, I was going to pubs and clubs, drinking and smoking. Peers enticed me with weed at the age of fifteen. My Anorexia and hormones, mixed with these toxins, allowed me to do what I liked in my own way. I earned my own money and felt that Mum tried everything to disrupt my life when, in fact, she was trying to save me.

4 | My Battle with Eating

I'd always been a fussy eater. Mum said I would decline food as a young child and spend time at the table once everyone had finished because I refused to eat. Was this compliance, or was I not hungry?

At age two, Mum threw a bowl of cornflakes over my head because, once again, I refused to eat, which made Liam late for school. I'd sit at the dinner table by age five, playing with food with everyone else present. It was usual for me to sit at that table, but it was unusual for half a bottle of wine to be left there. So, very quietly, I drank the wine and pretended to eat. Eating when I wasn't hungry felt unnatural, so why did I have to sit there? So, instead, I drank the wine. After a while, my parents noticed I was quiet. I had fallen asleep at the table.

It wasn't unusual for me to take people's drinks. My Nan used to give me Shebbys and Cinzano, so I wasn't left out, and it was a weakened version of the drinks. I ate when I wanted to, and she cooked me what I liked. I wasn't fat or thin, but very doll-like and cute. During family celebrations, I used to steal drinks and sip them when grown-ups placed them on the floor. After a while, I was asleep behind the sofa. Nobody was alarmed by it; this was me - a little cow.

I sucked my thumb until the age of ten, so my teeth stuck out, and I wet the bed until I was seven years old. My only identity was as 'Liam's little sister' and at home, I felt football was considered a priority. I was fat with tree trunk legs. That may be my early perception, but I looked and acted like a boy.

Holidays as a child were nonexistent; we went once to Clacton in a caravan. It pissed down every day, and days out related to finding a pub somewhere and sitting outside. My mum used to take us on day trips with my cousin or a family friend, Jack, with his kids Matt and Louise. Louise became my best childhood friend, and hated football too! My Dad never liked the idea of going abroad or enjoyed doing normal things with his kids. He loved his football, the pub and betting.

At about the age of eleven, I noticed everyone at school, including Louise, was growing boobs. I was the smallest in the class, resembling a ball with a flat chest. I was called "pimples" by my brother and "tree trunks" by my Dad. I was rubbish at sports and tried hard to impress my Dad at netball. Another parent commented on who the little fat girl with the tree trunk legs was. Although I know he loved me, I never felt Dad was very proud of me.

The only control I felt was with food. I went on various diets from the age of eleven to fourteen. I stopped eating in front of people, bathed a lot and had very hot baths as it burnt the calories. I wanted breasts like the other girls at school, and no matter how I padded my bra, they looked fake in the changing room. My hair became brittle, and my skin was spotty through lack of nutrients, but I was in control. I began to look at myself and saw a fat, ugly cow, but I was actually becoming a skeleton. So, I withdrew from school, and when I went out with my friends, I wore baggy tracksuits and lived on fags. If an adult forced me to eat, I threw up, and the thinner I became, the better I looked.

I was repulsed by the inner and outer me; the only other person who saw this was my mum. She pleaded with me to attend GP appointments, and I went. She was offered a psychiatric setting for me but knew I would refuse any intervention. It was different in those days. She could not bear the thought of her daughter attached to a drip. Food and my mum were my enemies. She knew when I was sick, and we constantly argued. She never gave up and always encouraged me to buy new clothes. Maybe she wanted me to look in the mirror to see how emaciated I had become, but I only saw a fat girl. I recognised how hard it must have been for my Mum to watch her daughter disappearing each day, becoming weaker but moving away from her control.

At the age of fourteen, I was 5'9 and six stone. Mum was helpless and tried so hard to help me by cooking food and buying clothes. By this time, I wasn't seeing my Nan and Grandad as much, and I started drinking and smoking and going to clubs and pubs. I worked in a clothes shop and had three paper rounds because I liked the money and clothes that used to hang off my skeletal frame, but I felt in control. The drink provided an escape. I was never at home and only went to have my hot baths. I was abusive to my mum, and my dad, well, he was always down the pub. Mum was my best friend at the time, but she felt like my enemy. I did not want this control removed by anyone. I knew best.

At sixteen, I went to work in a solicitor's office. I worked like a dog for those bastards, never having lunch breaks and working until seven in the evening. During this time, I was fainting a lot, and my periods, which I had only had for a year, stopped. I went on the pill to regulate them, and people told me that I'd grow breasts by taking it. I still had nothing, wore a padded bra and had only started really growing pubic hair. I looked like an eleven-year-old with a face full of makeup and big hair. My only experience of boys was a kiss at a party, and he said I had a chest like an ironing board and left me alone at Walthamstow station at midnight one Sunday evening. So yes, I had plenty of friends, I made everyone laugh, and I was fun. But nobody was attracted to me; they liked the girls who had bumps in their jumpers and had the confidence to have sex with boys.

5 | Kasey

I can't remember how I met Kasey, but we started going out drinking. Kasey was the attractive one who got the boys, especially the ones I used to fancy. Her house was a filthy hovel, but her mum and dad were always nice to me. I went home to wash as she didn't have a bathtub, but I always felt welcome.

I was about seven stone at seventeen, and her mum used to try to make me eat. Her dad always commented about how I looked. Leggings were in fashion, and my legs looked like sticks, but he used to say, "What a lovely shape you are; you look so tiny" and smack his lips. You can guess where he was looking. I used to feel uncomfortable with his comments, and I hated the smell of her house but adored her mum.

When I was sixteen, one boy used to wait for me at the bus stop after work and sit with me. He said he wanted me to be his girlfriend, so I avoided him and changed jobs. Kasey informed me a year later that she had fucked him in an alleyway. I was hurt and never understood if he liked me; he fucked her - but bless him, he really tried to convince me to be his girlfriend. He bought me my first Valentine's card.

At the age of seventeen, I went out with someone called Mark for two weeks, but when his hands started moving on my bum, I packed him in. He was far too forward for my liking, and it felt so uncomfortable when he tried to touch me.

I started to become attractive to men. Kasey and I went on holiday, but she was the one who did sexual things while I just gave the odd kiss. I never went further than a kiss. Back at home, men in the pub asked me out and bought me drinks, but I was standoffish and told them to fuck off. I was a laughing stock. My dad had shown his affection by taking the piss out of me, which he found funny. I knew he loved me but had a very strange way of showing it. I don't think this helped me in my forming relationships with the opposite sex.

I would lash out while we were out if I had too much attention from men who wouldn't leave me alone or expected a kiss or more at the end of the evening. I then received fat lips from people or got spat at when I told them to leave me alone.

"What's wrong with you, Kasey puts out?"

Then, when I went home with a fat lip, my dad would find out who did it. I'm not sure what happened afterwards, and I never asked; I was too busy planning the next night out with Kasey. I expected men to be nasty if I refused them, especially when they were full of drink. I became a target because I said no. Then it happened.

Kasey was going home with one of Marks's friends, I pleaded with her not to go with him, but she wanted to fuck him, and we would get a cab home. Mark had two other friends with him. We all walked home together, and Mark tried to kiss me and ask me to be his girlfriend. I said no.

Kasey was walking ahead with Mike. Suddenly, Mark threw me over a fence from nowhere and pulled my dress up. I screamed for Kasey to help me once, then froze. I saw a penis in my face, so I couldn't open my mouth, and I felt someone kneeling over my head.

Mark undid his trousers and said, "You're frigid bitch", and he slapped his penis in my face.

"Open your fucking mouth bitch", and then I saw a hand wanking over my head. He was going to cum over my face.

I lay there frozen; I could not fight if I opened my mouth. Mark was on top of me. My underwear was down to my knees, but my knees were closed together. I could feel his friend panting over me. I couldn't think; I just kept everything closed and tight. Kasey had run off. I was alone and about to get violated by three boys. It felt like hours but was probably only a few seconds.

"Open your mouth, you're a fucking bitch!" Mark yelled at me.

"Don't cum yet; wait for me to have her mouth!" Mark continued to shout at his friend this time.

"Get your fucking legs open so I can get these off! You think you can say no to me?" Mark yelled in my face.

I shut my eyes; what else could I do - fight or flight?

Then suddenly, I heard a different voice.

"Get the fuck off of her!"

Mike had come back. He had heard my only scream. He pushed them all away, and I managed to get my clothes straightened. Mark then cruelly laughed at me while Kasey was nowhere to be seen. Mike got me a cab, and it took me home. Nobody would ever touch me like that again.

My waning eating disorder came back with a vengeance. Kasey had betrayed me, and I found some new friends. But my substitution was now drugs - cannabis and speed, plus my daily intake of cigarettes. I hated my body, I hated men, I hated Kasey, and I hated my Mum; everyone was trying to control me with food. Do this, do that, eat this, try that. Fuck off, world, you haven't a clue how I feel. If I died, no one would miss me except Grandad. I told no one; I just turned off my feelings and rejected the hunger. I actually liked it, mutilating the body that everybody laughed at or tried to violate. I hated the world. But most of all, I wanted to love something one day, something of mine that nobody could control or take away from me. I resisted the choice of killing myself to become someone's mummy.

6 | Star Struck

The only person who came close to his hand going inside my knickers was Warren. I met him in a pub when I was out with the girls. He was tall, muscular, and blond, like a young Dolph Lundgren. He was described by my friends as a "top sort". Word got out that he liked me, and how could you not refuse this geezer.

His ex-girlfriend, however, used to drink at a local pub. She was everything I was not, curvy, enormous tits and bright blonde hair fastened in a banana comb. She wore tight lycra dresses that really emphasised her curves. I thought she looked sexy, so every man on this planet must have felt the same. Whereas I was very slim, had no boobs, was tall, leggy and had very pointy features. I had been to some modelling agencies and had a portfolio; I was the shape of a catwalk model and had the bone structure of one. It was the age of Kate Moss and the supermodels. Some people said I was like some well-known TV and model personalities. I just used to shake off compliments and still find it hard to accept them today.

Warren asked me out, and we would go to clubs and pubs; he knew some of our crowd, so he really fitted in. He had a car, so he used to pick me up. I met his mum, she liked me and said I was beautiful and better than the other tart he had been with for three years. But Warren was used to a sexual relationship, and I only gave him a kiss at the end of the night. He would put my hand to his groin, but immediately, I would withdraw it. There's no way I was touching his cock. After six months, he started to talk about his ex, saying that he missed the physical side of it, and after kissing one night on my mum's sofa, he tried to put his fingers inside my knickers. I pushed him away.

"For God's sake, J, I am a man. It's been six months."

"And? Well, fuck off back to her then," I cried.

During a phone conversation, he said he wanted to be with me but needed sex. My mum came into the room, telling me to leave it and let him go. He went back to her for a few months, but she cheated on him.

I really did not know anything about sex. Yes, I got fuzzy when I kissed a good kisser, but there have been times I have been physically sick when being kissed like a washing machine , with a tongue going round and round in my mouth. All I did was kiss, and after nearly getting raped a couple of years before, I wanted to wait until I found Mr. Right. My friends were always shagging different blokes; I didn't quite understand why, though?

I was a virgin when I met Jimmy; and first met him in an old High Beech, Essex pub. A pub which, at the time, I thought was out of my league. It was full of blondes in lycra dresses, big bouncy hair, fantastic figures, with cleavage popping out of their tiny clothing.

And there was me - all in black: mini skirt, knee-high suede boots and a jacket with my hair in a side ponytail. I wore nothing I felt was elaborate, nothing eye-catching, as I did not want anyone to notice me. And why would they look at someone who had no tits, wasn't wearing designer brands and had hair that wasn't at all blonde?

Now, my friends at that time were not shy about men. As I was the only virgin and they were all on thirty-plus numbers, it gave me security at the end of the night; they would be the ones fucking, and at least one of them would be going home with a boy or taking a home phone number as the bare minimum. By the way, we did not have mobile phones then; you waited by the telephone for that call for at least two days and then gave up. They always got the call back as they had promised them a shag.

There was a large group of us, but often we went out in twos or threes. Sharon and Hannah were up for it most, and I was amazed at their confidence. Sharon had tiny boobs too, but always managed to make the most of her appearance. She loved tiger skin clothes, leggings, and little skirts. Despite that, she was a bit bandy on the legs. But Sharon was lovely, did not have a filter, but was stupid and never malicious.

Hannah was sexy; she had short hair, enormous tits but just oozed sex. She knew what she wanted and got the boy at the end of the night. She wasn't loud, but when she fixed her eyes on someone, she used her sexual allure to get them in her bed. She never cared if they were married or had a long-term girlfriend. Hannah had a fantastic job in the city, a mortgage, always had money, but was never flash with it. However, she could never hold down a man for more than one night. She used them as much as they used her.

Anyway, on this night, the pub was blaring out eighties tunes, and we were all getting pissed even though Sharon was driving. The pub was packed, INXS was playing, and suddenly, the pub was separated; there was a big opening. I laughed and joked at Hannah and Sharon, who were eyeing the latest prey.

"C'mon Ju, you can't stay a virgin forever! You need some action," they mocked.

I was fine being a virgin; I did not want anyone to touch me again after what had happened with Warren and Mark. Nope, boys were not on the agenda, and I was not interested in girls either; Megan had also put a stop to that.

This was until Sharon said, "Ju, Jimmy Parker is staring at you!"

It was a bit like Moses when the sea parted, and I saw these two brown eyes just bearing into my soul. Jimmy Parker, who? Nope, he wasn't looking at me; there was a big buxom blonde beside me, and there was Sharon and Hannah. Why would this gorgeous creature look at the plain, leggy, skinny Jane? I ignored him and said he was not looking at me. I turned my back and reverted my attention to the latest victim of Hannah, pleading with her to find someone single.

But no, Hannah loved it if the boy was with his girl, holding her hands. Hannah felt this was a challenge, so she would catch his eye by pressing out her chest. I can only describe it as the Bisto kids advert; the man smelt the allure, saw the breasts pushed out and then gave the nod to Hannah. Delighted by her achievement, Hannah would then go to the bar, and he would follow.

"I'm just going to the bar; where's Sharon?"

Sharon was in the toilet, probably chatting to someone, leaving me alone in the crowded pub. I would not follow Hannah to the bar and encourage the next stage of her performance. I would watch his girlfriend to see if she noticed what was happening and then work out if it would turn nasty. Hannah could handle herself, where Sharon's high-pitched voice would go higher, and then there would be a scene. Yes, this was a regular occurrence; I was the mediator who would reason with an irate girl, trying to explain the same old story my friend thought she knew him from the train every morning. Then I'd apologise and say she must have got it wrong before I dragged Hannah or Sharon away. We would leave, or there would be a slanging match in the car park, possibly a row, and then have a good laugh about it on the way home.

While Hannah was at the bar, Sharon was in the loo, and the girlfriend was chatting away, oblivious to her boyfriend's hand up Hannah's skirt. I was very good at ignoring the obvious.

Then, something caught my eye; Jimmy was smiling, looking straight at me. Once again, I thought it couldn't be me, so I ignored him. The voice close to me became louder and louder; I looked up and saw a pair of dark stone eyes looking at me.

"Are you ignoring me?"

Huh, I looked around for Hannah and Sharon; oh fuck, here we go; who the fuck was this? Some drunk fucker who thought he would try his luck?

"Oi," and I felt a poke in my side.

Who the fuck was touching me? As I turned round to confront the guy, feeling slightly confused, I saw the girlfriend was still within my range. And Hannah was still up at the bar with her lad.

I suddenly saw a tanned god standing directly in front of me. OMG, he looked like the spitting image of a famous pop star. I immediately turned back away; it must have been a mistake. Oh shit, I felt my face glowing. Calm down, Ju; where the fuck was someone when you need them? I had no one to talk to and felt very vulnerable. Hannah was now snogging, and the guy was touching her up more at the bar. Where was Sharon?

Suddenly, I felt another poke, "oi".

Now I was getting pissed off; I really didn't care about this pop star, whatever you want to call him, chatting up the bird next to me. He could fuck off and take this bird somewhere else. I turned round to tell him to fuck off when I got transfixed on those beautiful brown eyes. His mouth moved, but I refused to listen; I realised he was talking to me, not the blonde. Had I got something on my face? Was there a bet with his mates to pull the flattest-chested woman in the pub?

"Do you want a drink? Why are you ignoring me? I have been trying to get your attention for the past half hour," he said.

Half an hour - is that how long they have left me? Fucking bitches, and now I must deal with this shit on my own, with Jake, Jimmy, whatever his fucking name is. I was swearing as I was feeling a bag of nerves.

"No, I'm fine, thanks."

Or should I say, "Brandy and Babycham?" That would serve him right for playing this bet. A Brandy and Babycham would cost a fortune in this pub.

"Yeh, okay, I'll have a Brandy and Babycham please".

Yep, now fuck off, Jimmy and leave me alone, I need to find Sharon, she knows him. She can chat with him.

Fortunately, I heard a voice: Sharon - she had seen this from a distance. And then I thought about my escape. I couldn't deal with this man; he'd already tried to poke me, and he may try to kiss me, thinking I was like them. I don't just kiss anyone! Omg!

"I am just going outside with Adam; you okay, Jim, with Julia?" asked Sharon.

Who the fuck was Adam? Where are you going? Don't leave me with him, I don't know him! I couldn't get my words out quickly enough when she walked out with this ginger boy. Obviously, she would be back in five, ten or twenty minutes - but that felt a lifetime. I looked across at Hannah; she had her tongue down a random boy's throat. I was not even looking at where his hands were. Why did I go out with just these two? Why does this happen to me every time we go out? They pull or fuck or whatever you want to call it, and I was then left watching for trouble.

So, Jimmy said, "Are you coming then to the bar?"

What else could I do? What were my options? I was being hypnotised to the bar by this lookalike famous singer. I was star-struck, and let's be honest, a couple of lookalike famous footballers and actors had asked me out before and since. Only twice have I been star-struck, and this was one of the occasions.

We were at the bar; it was packed, but he managed to get a drink before anyone else. There were a few comments, but he told them to fuck off. Nobody challenged him, but I was caught up in the moment. Me, 'no tits', was at the bar with the best-looking man in the place, and he was a man, he was in his late twenties. This man wanted to buy me a drink and talk to me when all these beautiful, big, busted women with perfect hair and makeup were in the same pub.

I don't know what we spoke about; all I could see was his smile. He never touched me inappropriately, but I was locked in his eyes, and that's all that mattered. His hair was dark brown, spiky, with big sideburns and a bit of stubble. He was tanned, his face had a few laughter lines, and he had very thin lips and a broad chin. I am telling you this was as close to the star you could get. Then, what happened? Bloody Sharon came over and grabbed Hannah at the bar.

"We've got to go. It's going to kick off; Adam's girlfriend is here".

Huh! I was then in her car; I'd been all warm with Brandy and Babycham talking to a star, well, not talking, dreaming with a star, and now I was fucking well sat in a cold car smelling of sex and fags. This was not how the night should have ended. I was not laughing at Hannah and Sharon's exploits tonight; I felt cheated.

7 | Georgina

After meeting Jimmy in that pub, he contacted my friend Sharon and said he wanted to take me out. I wanted to look good that day and had a long sunbed. It fucking burnt my face, so I went to the date looking like a roasted dry peanut. He laughed when he picked me up.

"What the fuck's wrong with your face?"

Jimmy had borrowed his work truck; I was so proud to be with him, and we went to a pub in Chingford, Essex. He made me laugh, and it felt nice when he kissed me at the end of the night. So, we arranged to meet again.

Jimmy had this ex who would not leave him alone. She was an ugly little frigger but put out in bed. She was very blonde with large tits and a face that only a mother could love. She was really fucking ugly... I went out with him for about two months when Sharon came to pick me up, and I asked if I could pop in and see Jimmy to drop something off. He was lodging with an older woman he used to fuck. I was friends with her daughter, so we picked her up. I noticed a car on the drive when I got to the door. It was fucking Miss Piggy; he came downstairs and explained to me that she wanted to get back with him. I said to go for it. Then, I turned my back and walked to Sharon's car.

My friend came running out and said, "It's not Jimmy's fault, J; he told her he's seeing you."

"Get in the car," said Sharon. "C'mon, we are late".

By the age of nineteen, I was with Jimmy, smoking and taking drugs. I was a virgin when Jimmy forced himself inside me. After that, I really hated sex; I just laid there like a sack of potatoes, waiting for him to get inside me, no kissing; he said that I couldn't fuck or suck his cock properly.

Before I entered any establishment, I was told to walk in with my head down and not talk to anyone except Jimmy. On the evening Grandad died, we were out drinking in a pub when Mum managed to get a message to me that I was needed at the hospital. My last words with Grandad were lovingly told before leaving the hospital - 'I looked an old tart wearing that rubber skirt and skimpy top.' I was painting my nails at his bedside, and he was chatting away to me. I left the hospital to meet our friends and have a good drink.

Later that night I got the call; one of my friends had managed to get to the pub to tell me. I immediately rushed to the hospital and through to the ward. The nurse tried to stop me, but I pushed her away and went to the bed. Grandad was lying there with a bandage tied around his chin to stop him from drooping.

Mum said, "He's gone, Ju."

I ran out of the ward and screamed at the top of my voice outside the grounds. Hysterical, I started to kick and punch out at anyone who approached me. I wanted Jimmy, but he hadn't come with me; he was back at the pub regardless of how I felt. My Mum then told me to go. I felt so alone at that moment. All I could think about was that amazing man who had left me and cried out for the man to whom I needed to express my grief; instead, he used it to hurt me. I am unsure where I slept that night, and I can't remember what happened the next day, but I needed something that was mine and could love. It would be easy to replace this void with a baby. Everything and everyone would stop hurting me once I had someone to love.

I got home one day, angry at my Grandad for dying, raging at the world for taking this man away from me and upset as I felt no one else was mourning him. I came in like a whirlwind and started shouting and swearing. Sitting in the chair, my brother got up and grabbed me by the neck; I was halfway up the wall in seconds. I was spluttering and choking until Mum told him to let go. She then said she could not cope with me anymore, and I had to go.

I grieved my beloved Grandfather, I'd lost the most magical man in my life. A person that I trusted and loved beyond all measures. My Nan was also mourning him and wanted company, so I went to stay with her. Jimmy lived just around the corner, so I went to work and cook or buy dinner for my Nan, and then I would go to Jimmy's. Nan felt that I should have stayed with her; I never considered her feelings about losing her husband. I did not have the maturity to understand her loss; all I felt was my pain and how Jimmy and the baby I wanted could make it disappear. Grandad had never liked Jimmy, said he was a 'wrong un' and he was lodging with an old tart at the time. I listened to him but never took his advice.

I stayed at my Nan's for a short while, and then my Mum managed to get me a room in a shared house around the corner. I hated her for this and felt even more isolated. I relied totally on Jimmy; I thought nobody else loved me. I felt rejected and hurt by all my family. I did not talk to my brother for eighteen months or my Mum for at least three. I felt she picked him over me; he should have been punished for hurting me. I could not see the real picture of me being a perpetrator, while crying out for help as I was in my own bitter world. I was now totally in Jimmy's control. I was a mess, but I believed I was on top of the world; no one, not even my friends, could advise me. I hit out, shouted and ignored any advice. He became my world and my protector. He loved me. I abandoned my family to be with him.

I lived in a very cold room twenty miles away from Jimmy, so I rarely stayed with him. The downstairs of my lodgings was a business, so I felt uncomfortable as the business owner's son was often there. He stayed late in the evening and often slept on the couch. My friends bought me a mouse to keep me company and to show how cold the room was; it eventually froze to death.

One night, Jimmy and I decided to come back to the room. My quilt had been removed from my room, and we found the owner's son asleep under it. Jimmy went ballistic, asking how often he came into my room and smacked the bloke in the mouth. My door had been locked, and I protested my innocence. The quilt stealer was shocked and had blood running from his mouth. He stood there and said nothing. Jimmy then pushed me against the wall and told me to get upstairs. He then pulled my skirt up and knickers down and came inside me. He then zipped up his jeans and walked out of the house.

What the fuck just went on? I somehow believed it was my fault, got into my car and tried to follow Jimmy at speed. I remember the song playing was a Lisa Mansfield track with very apt words about finding someone - and I did. I said I was so sorry. Then he forced himself into me, and I apologised for somebody else breaking into my room and stealing my quilt. I let him fuck me again, as I at least owed him that. As I broke the rules by allowing my boyfriend in my room, my landlord evicted me and gave me a couple of days to get out. He also said I was lucky that I was not prosecuted for his son's injury. I did not protest; I had no choice but to live with Jimmy, and guess what? I was pregnant.

We had the funeral, and Jimmy turned up late. I was furious with him, but it just wasn't the right time to have a row. My family were all together in the main car, feeling so sad, but there was a funny moment in the car going to the funeral when my hold-ups fell down. My Grandad would have laughed at my embarrassment but then hugged me and said, 'Toffee, you need to eat more.' My legs were so skinny then that nothing really fitted well. I was six and a half stone then, and at 5'9, I was in no fit state to have a baby. But Jimmy encouraged the pregnancy.

We were so excited about having a baby. Jimmy was several years older than me, so he was ready. Mum was worried as I was so underweight, and I was staying in a single room with Jimmy at his lodgings. He previously had a relationship with his landlady, who was twenty years older than him. The explanation was that he was treated like her son, and I was friends with her daughter Jodie.

One night, our friendship group were all drinking, and I suddenly felt a strange pain in my stomach. I went upstairs to the toilet and found blood as I wiped myself. I went downstairs and told my friends. Jimmy was out, and so my friends took me to the hospital. I had not been drinking, but Jimmy's behaviour during the pregnancy had been appalling. He had become so jealous that I was relieved he wasn't there. I told myself that if it was just nothing, he wouldn't have to know about it, as he'd blame me. The verdict was that I was miscarrying and needed to go home and rest. Nature would take its course, and as I was in the early stages, it would happen naturally. Nobody told me about the pain I would experience, and nobody told me about Jimmy's explosive reaction when I returned home.

When I entered through the door, my friend Lena told him to calm down as he was mad.

"Where the fuck have you been?"

Lena explained that I had been to the hospital and that I was in the process of losing the baby. He then grabbed me by the throat and threatened that I did not tell him due to him not being the baby's father. I needed to sit down; I was crying; all I wanted was my mum, but I felt too ashamed to go to her. He slapped my face and told me to "fuck off with the father".

I pleaded with him that he was the father, but he wouldn't listen; he lifted me up and literally threw me out of the door "fucking slag".

Lena waited outside for me, as you never confronted Jimmy when he was mad.

"Ju come home with me."

However, I was tired and adamant that he would listen, so I begged him to let me in. He eventually let me in, and I promised never to lie to him again. I had tried to protect him in my misery, but he turned it around to make out I had lied. Stupidly, I accepted his punishment. He made me sleep on the floor, where I bled and lost the baby. I was nineteen when I suffered my first loss. After that, we planned to have more children.

It was the recession of 1990. I was pregnant again, and we were told we had to leave Jimmy's friend's flat. So, we went down to the council and said we were homeless. They offered us a hotel room that night. It was in Finsbury Park around the red-light district. When we entered the run-down hovel, it was more like a drug den than a hotel; I cried when I saw it. The wallpaper was peeling off; there was dampness in the corners of the room. The bed looked ready for the skip, and I couldn't bear to even look at the mattress as it screamed of semen and bed bugs. The toilet had no seat, and there was excrement around the sides of the bowl. The sink was stained with limescale and filth, and the shower was a box with a stained shower curtain. We did not turn the shower on. To top it all, they wanted £145.00 per night for that shit hole. Jimmy was working as a builder, making some money, but it was unfit for purpose.

"Ju, get your arse out of this fucking hole, we are not staying here."

So, we stayed in his van. I never slept a wink but wasn't scared as Jimmy could look after us. He often got paid for bare-knuckle fighting but promised to never fight again. Well, not for money. All night, I watched the sex workers go back and forth on the streets; there were a couple of fights and a pair of drunks tapped on the window of the van. Jimmy told them to fuck off and had to get out of the van once. No one messed around with Jimmy - but that impressed me as I felt protected.

The next morning, we returned to the council; we hadn't washed, and not having a bath triggered and bothered me. Since I was little, one of my habits for my eating disorder was to have at least two hot baths a day. It helped me release tension, reduce calories and feel clean. We waited at that office all day and refused to leave until they allocated us somewhere different. All our belongings were in the van: an old television, our clothes, a box containing a kettle, saucepan, cups and plates, etc. We had a double duvet sheet, and I made sure before leaving his mate's flat, I scrubbed it inside out and cleaned all our clothes and bed linen.

We were given a hostel in Palmers Green, North London. It was made from two huge houses made into one place. It was another room shared with thirty other families. There were three bathrooms and a toilet. So I would have to get up early and again late at night to get clean. There wasn't a washing machine, so I would use the bath to clean our clothes. Jimmy was a builder but expected his white vests to be white. If there was a stain, I would be made to rewash it and get called a useless cunt. The kitchen was shared, and we were allocated a cupboard. The other occupants were either Asian or Turkish; no other white people were living there. It was very poor housing conditions and was impossible to cook a meal there. I used to scrub that kitchen, but it never felt clean, and Jimmy refused to eat there. So, we had a camping stove and cooked basic food until he obtained a microwave. Do not ask me how; with Jimmy, you never asked questions else you were told to mind your own fucking business.

After three weeks, we were allocated another room in Palmers Green. We shared it with three other families: a Scottish couple, a single mum with a boyfriend who had just come out of prison, and there was a family downstairs. We lived there for nine months, had no central heating and sometimes no hot water. Jimmy couldn't find work, and we were not eligible for benefits.

I became friends with the single mum, Gina; she was lovely. She was brought up by decent parents but found herself loving a scum bag. He was a compulsive liar and went AWOL for days and weeks, leaving her to look after herself. She was still working and often helped us with food when we had nothing. Gina also saw a lot of Jimmy's violence towards me. She watched me cut his food up for him, make sure his dinner was ready at a specific time, and scrub his white vests in the bath even though I was heavily pregnant. She watched him call me a 'useless cunt' and a 'dirty bitch' if I failed to keep up with the cleaning regime or dinner was not on time. Gina often told Jimmy not to call me that; I didn't deserve it. Unfortunately, whenever Jimmy heard her comment, I would get hit for talking to her about him.

Jimmy and I were watching TV one night when we heard a sudden bang. A police officer came up the stairs shouting at Gina's door. She stood shaking while they searched her room and threw all her new, clean baby items over the floor. She was distraught, so we told her to come into our room. Obviously, her man was on one of his holidays. He would return looking like a vagrant, but she always took him back. Apart from the odd dig and name-calling, I was lucky.

The Scottish couple had left the hostel in a hurry. Jimmy suspected they still had something in their room we could use. There was no heating, and it was freezing, so he broke into the room and took a heater. He climbed from our window onto the ledge and smashed his way in. Gina could not believe it and laughed hysterically. Her room was tiny, so it kept the heat. We had a larger room, but there was no insulation around the windows, so it was draughty and it had recently snowed. We lived on a road littered with rubbish and filthy corner shops stacked with boxes and boxes of rotting vegetables. There was a mosque nearby, so I used to watch the men going to pray, and there were sounds of prayer amongst the dirty fog of pollution caused by the ongoing traffic. It was such an unhealthy place to be pregnant. Gina and I kept the upstairs clean, keeping each other company when Jimmy was out, and her man was away.

"Who have you been talking to? What have you two whores been doing today?" sneered Jimmy quite regularly after he'd been out.

Gina told me that she heard the slaps and muffled screams when Jimmy got me by the throat.

He would shout out, "I told you; you are mine - you're a fucking disgrace!"

I'd say I was sorry and wouldn't do it again, and then he would fuck me.

"I love you; I didn't mean it; I just get jealous. Just don't talk to other men," he'd reply.

Apart from shopping, the only person I spoke to was Gina. There were no mobile phones. The only break I got was on a Saturday when my mum would come and get me. I couldn't tell her what was going on. Also, Liam had my old room with his fiancée as they were saving to get married and buy a home.

One cold morning, we really had nothing. I had previously sold cigarette cards in frames to try to get money for food. Mum had paid towards the rent arrears as we'd been threatened with eviction. Jimmy had not worked for weeks, so I went down to the old flea shop and said I had some furniture to sell. We had a wardrobe and chest of drawers from the council. The man asked for my address.

He laughed and said, "Gel, I sold it to the council. Now go home".

That night, we laughed over a bowl of soup with Gina, who had once again bought the food. After a sarcastic comment I made, Jimmy decided to dangle me over the balcony with one hand, until Gina screamed to put me down. To this day, I am frightened of heights; it makes me feel physically sick and takes me back to that moment. I had no control or say, and I refused to beg for safety.

Now Jimmy was a proud man, and he hated Gina giving us food, but he would not go to his family for help, and I knew my mum would say to leave him. I loved him as he loved me. I was having his baby; I couldn't sleep with another man. I made the promise to my unborn child I would give it as much love as I could. I did not know about the impact of domestic abuse on the unborn child as it wasn't spoken about. My pregnancy consisted of his obsessive, jealous behaviour, demanding sex every night, and I had to wear kinky clothes as he said it was covering my fat bump. I did not show until I was seven months pregnant, so thinking about it now, it was all about control. I was wearing miniskirts and he bought me over-the-knee boots that he would make me wear in front of his friends to show off my long legs. They were high and totally inappropriate for the day, but it was easier to wear them. I would also get hit if anyone commented on them. Not in front of his friends. The silent punches under the sheets, pinches and prods, reminding me that I was his. He never touched my face; he used to strangle me if I refused to have sex with him, but I was in this situation, and there was no going back. I wanted his baby, I wanted him, and I thought I deserved the abuse he gave me. He made me put bright lipstick and a full face of make-up on for him while he was in and then accused me of sleeping around when I went out looking nice. I couldn't win.

One day, Jimmy wanted to buy some fish from a local seafood stall, and he told me to get out of the car and get it. I got out, and a man asked me the time. I told him, turning to Jimmy, who clocked the man talking.

When I got in the car, he said, "You can't help yourself, you are fucking slag!" and punched me in the stomach.

I cried as it hurt, thinking he was killing my baby. All he did was go on and on about me being a fucking slag and a cunt. What could I do? I did not want to admit to anyone what was going on. So, I pretended to be happy, and he made me feel it was my fault.

The night Georgina was born was Jimmy's father's birthday. I had contractions one particular evening, and the midwife told me to stay in the hospital when I got myself examined. Later, my waters broke, and I was alone as Jimmy had gone back to the room. My mum managed to get hold of a friend for me an hour and a half before she was born. Meanwhile, Jimmy had a bath, shaved, put on his aftershave, was in no rush, and came to the hospital after complaining that he had to make his coffee and food. By this time, I was in heavy labour; a huge pain rushed through my body, and I screamed.

"Shut the fuck up," he said.

Georgina was born. My beautiful little girl.

See in the distance a view standing so morose
Chuffing away on a roll up alone in a cloud
That vision of pure splendour
The aura of hope that time remains still

I've been cheated with a regal tone
All I have is the taste and memory of perfection, possibly fiction
The inner voice screaming
My thoughts stay within
The tyres move, and the smoke has faded

I'm left with a longing, the residue of intimacy,
Safety is key,

It won't be long till I get the message of hope
The feeling of warmth, penetration deep beyond embracing the scars of despair
That the sun shines again in my heart

8 | Poverty in One Room

After having Georgina, when it came to sex, I just had to lay on my back, and Jimmy fucked me. If he turned me over, then he was too big, and I just couldn't take him all. I couldn't even do that properly. I didn't give a shit; I fucking hated sex; it made me smell, he was not gentle, and he made me feel like a piece of meat. I would do anything to get out of having sex with him. I would take the odd kick or punch as that would be much quicker and easier than washing out that vile smell as he stunk.

One day, as usual, he was timing how long I had been out shopping.

Georgina was a baby, and he said, "You're late, right, you need to sit down. I have something for you to watch."

I did not have enough time to put the shopping away when he made me sit in front of the television crossed-legged. He put a video in the recorder. Suddenly, on the screen, there was this strange music and a woman dressed in a maid costume; a man walked into the room and started to kiss her and put his hand up her dress, and she started moaning.

I turned around and said, "What?"

He turned my head back sharply and said, "Fucking watch it. You're fucking useless, and you're going to watch it."

I watched him grab her tits and start fucking her.

"See, you're supposed to move."

He then cum over her face. Well, I was gagging at the thought of that. Every day I was forced to watch porn, lesbian orgies, and the situation just got worse. I just was not interested. He would comment about how big the lesbians' tits were and how pathetic my tits were. And how beautiful they looked, not like a fat piece of lard just lying there. However, it gave me an insight into what men wanted in bed. Although he would never experience this benefit. I also once told him many years later he couldn't fuck to save his life.

I was sometimes made to dress up in suspenders and stockings and watch the porn cross-legged in front of the TV.

He would then uncross my legs and start fingering me while I was watching. I learnt how to make noises and how to wank like they did. He would get me to smoke pot so I could relax a bit more, and it wouldn't hurt me as much. If I didn't look like I was enjoying it, then I would get slapped and insulted; if I faked it and the stupid bastard couldn't tell, then I was told I was a fucking dirty slag. I felt humiliated and dressed up like a whore, but men, do like this sexy look and want a woman to dress up for them in the bedroom.

If I managed to go out with my friends, and they were only his friend's girlfriends, then just before I went out, he would pull my knickers down and fuck me and make me walk out with his cum running down my legs. If I came in late, I would be forced to have sex with him. I could not refuse as he would get spiteful and try to burn me with cigarettes and lighters. There was nothing to make a scar, but it singed the hair, so I knew he would be capable of doing more.

He would never use dildos on me as they made him feel inadequate, yet he used to tie me up so tight with scarfs or laces on my wrists and ankles it would burn into my skin. He would punish me by gagging me so I couldn't say no, then try and cut me just slightly with a razor, not so it bled, but I felt it. I was terrified of him, but something inside me just went along with it. I have scars all over my body because of him. He would strangle me, and then just as I was about to pass out, he would stop and then say, "I fucking love you. Why don't you love me?" I fucking hated him, but I thought I loved him at the same time. He was Georgina's dad and always said I would never escape him. Nobody would ever touch me as I was his property, his trophy. I was traumatised most of the time and I was Jimmy's fucking puppet in his very own sex show.

Living with Jimmy wasn't easy; he was very demanding personally and within the home. He expected the home to be spick and span. I used to dread the car pulling up and his footsteps coming up the stairs. I held my breath as I heard the key turn in the door. What mood was he going to be in? There would be trouble if I hadn't his dinner ready or if the flat was not clean enough.

Jimmy would do his daily routine, check every cupboard, and ensure the contents were placed in a clean and tidy order. If something was not in the right place, he would take it all out and make me clean it again. I had to cut up his food for him and watch to see if he would throw it against the wall or eat it without any sarcastic comments. If I was told, "That was nice cunt", then it would be something else. He would run his finger over the doors and skirting boards to see if there was any dust. My heavy net curtains were washed at least once a month, and our bed sheets were cleaned weekly. If there was a stain on the carpet or Georgina dropped food, I was booted in the leg. If a glass had a mark on it, then I was called a dirty cunt.

Nobody male was allowed to enter the house except my brother, who only visited me once or twice. His own family was not allowed in; if they popped around and he wasn't in, I expected a volume of questions and would be called a slag. I was not allowed to smile and converse without being accused of flirting. One night, he made me wear thigh-high boots to show off to his friend and then simulated bending me over to show him what he was missing. I felt humiliated and abused and had no self-esteem.

Washing had to be in the washing machine the same day, and he would inspect my ironing, making me do it repeatedly. The bathroom had to be shiny, and the kitchen had to be in immaculate order. Yet every night, his friends would come up, and I was expected to cook and clean before I went to bed. My lipstick would be wiped off first because that was for him only.

Sometimes, he would make me watch him clean. He said I had to stand there and watch him give me instructions to clean properly. He would flick the cloth in my face if I was not giving him my full attention. If he did not like the food I served, I was told to cook something else. Pizza was not a meal; it had to be meat and potatoes. He would check his plate if offered food, and I would get threatened if it looked like somebody else had the same amount. He was the alpha - so he was fed first and had the most.

9 | Lost Babies

A year after Georgina was born, I found out I was pregnant again. I wanted a brother or sister for her; Jimmy was dying for a son. He continued to be abusive physically and emotionally. He said I was a crap mother to Georgina; I was lazy and dirty. Georgina only slept a few hours during the day and was wide awake at night. I was tired and didn't want to have sex with him, but that never stopped him from forcing himself on me most nights.

Georgina slept in a cot in our room; by this time, the council had provided us with a two-bedroom flat. Jimmy insisted she slept in her cot, but Georgina was used to sleeping with me. She used to scream and scream once I placed her in the cot, and to get a couple of hours, I used to put her in bed with me.

Jimmy complained and used to kick me when she used to cry, so I would go into the lounge until she was asleep, as he would complain she was crying. I would get into bed and then try to sleep myself. He then used to wake up and paw me, spread my legs apart and then fuck me. After having sex with him, I used to smell of sex; I knew Georgina would wake up very soon, and I wanted her to lie next to me and not have that foul smell. He used to kick me out of bed, saying, "Go and wash you dirty cunt", and accuse me of having an affair. I would then get punched in the back and hips as he said he had no room and the baby was keeping him awake. You may ask why I wanted another baby, but my baby was my pride and joy, and I did not want her to be an only child and have no one to play with. His family would often ask why I was not pregnant again before they knew, as we didn't want a gap between them. He wanted four children. I was happy with another baby.

I never ate properly, as Jimmy would call me fat and ugly; he said that I had a big cunt, and I wasn't like a virgin. He would watch me exercise to tighten my tummy muscles, and I knew in my heart I wasn't fat. An eating disorder distorts your mind, so when you look in the mirror, you see a fat woman. Pregnancy made it worse, so I ate just enough not to faint. I looked pale, and I felt tired all the time. We still entertained his friends; they never considered that I was pregnant or needed to sleep. I cooked and made them drinks, always offering him first. If I made that mistake by offering to somebody else, he would punch me after they went home. He would accuse me of coming on to his friends and disrespecting him.

I lost this baby around six weeks again. I was shopping at Sainsbury's with Mum when I felt a warm sensation in my knickers. I never bothered going to the hospital and knew what to expect when Jimmy came home.

"You can't even keep a baby, can you? You're a useless cunt."

That was my name, "cunt ", he would say to Georgina, "Your mother is a cunt." Her pretty green eyes would just look at him. She would turn to me and put her chubby little arms up for a cuddle. I had her. That was all that mattered to me.

After the miscarriage, he became very violent. Every day, he punished me. It might be for Georgina spilling her milk, the flat wasn't tidy enough, or if she had chocolate around her face or outfit.

When Georgina was two, I managed to chuck Jimmy out of the flat. I explained that he needed to go away for a while if he wanted another baby. He went to live with his family. Every night, he would manage to slip in by the neighbour downstairs and call me names outside my door. He would cry and then beg me to let him in. He would bang on the door and wake up Georgina. The neighbour downstairs would let him in. We split for two months; I was getting pressure from his family to take him back. He promised me he would change, and I felt lonely.

Mum would try her best, but I lived in another part of London, and she worked full-time. We did not have a house phone, and I remember taking Georgina out to call a doctor and ask Mum for her help. I was exhausted and took him back.

Things were okay for a couple of weeks, and then I became pregnant again. I was ill throughout the pregnancy, and at fifteen weeks, I went for a scan. Jimmy went with me to the appointment and had Georgina on his lap. The nurse put the jelly on my abdomen and then walked out of the room after a few minutes. Another professional came in, did the same and then explained that my baby had died and the placenta was still growing. The medical term is a blighted ovum. They said the placenta would keep growing and sent me home, telling me to return the next day. I went home numb; he was quiet for once as it was a huge shock for him.

The next day, we had a glimmer of hope; the midwife said that I was expecting twins and the placenta must have hidden one. I was overjoyed but sad at the same time.

"Don't lose this one", threatened Jimmy.

He was over the shock.

"I better get a boy this time."

The next couple of days, I started bleeding, and the midwife said that I was at risk of losing the baby. She told me to rest, but he insisted that I keep up the cleaning regime; I was constantly sick and tired and started losing big clots of blood. We were rushed into the hospital when the doctor said that I had lost the second twin.

I wanted my mum, but he wouldn't let her accompany me that night. He took Georgina home while I had to stay overnight and have surgery to remove everything. I was hysterical, and I wanted to cuddle my baby.

Over the next three months, I had three procedures as I kept on bleeding. I would walk into a shop, and there would be a puddle of blood running down my leg. I was weak, suffering from migraines, tired and depressed. I kept losing what they called "retained products", but my body still thought it was pregnant.

I could not bear to be near Jimmy; the doctor told us to wait a while before trying again. I refused to have sex with him as I was so frightened of getting pregnant. He was spending more and more time downstairs with Laura. She pretended to be my friend and told me he used to come down and cry. I felt guilty, useless, weak and tired. The only person I cared about was my girl. I hated him touching me. I didn't want him near me. He started to drink, and then he raped me. I fell pregnant but lost it at six weeks. I did not want any more children. I wanted to be as far away from him as possible.

10 | Is This Love?

One evening, Jimmy invited friends to dinner. His friend's wife stayed with me while they went out for half an hour. I gave my friend and the children their food to eat. I would not dare eat before him, so I waited but felt embarrassed and angry. When they came through the door, I told them to sit down while tipping both dinners in the bin. His friend could not believe what had happened. He knew that Jimmy would explode and decided to make a quick exit. His wife apologised for leaving so soon and asked if I would be okay.

I said, "Yeh, go, and I'll catch up with you soon. Don't worry about me; I'll be fine. I said to her, "Hope you enjoyed your dinner," and laughed.

The moment they walked out of the door, I was dragged to the kitchen and made to get on my knees. I was kicked in the back and stomach, and my feet were stamped on.

"Get that food out of the bin cunt".

I refused, so he held my head in the bin and told me to eat the contents. If I opened my mouth, then I would taste the rubbish. I just prayed that it would stop soon. Georgina was watching a video and came into the kitchen asking for a drink.

"Mummy, why are you in the bin?"

He pulled me by the hair; I had the residue of rubbish, fag ends, and ash on my face, and gravy splashed on my nose with florets of cauliflower.

"Your mother is a cunt, and she thinks she's funny!"

He made me clean the whole kitchen that night and inspected it before bed. Then I was turned on my front, told to get on my knees while he forced his way into me, holding my head down in the pillow.

"Think you can win cunt? I'm stronger than you!" he sneered.

I wanted to cry, but any tears for him had dried up a long time ago. I just wanted my baby in my arms and to feel clean again. After it had finished, he refused to let me clean myself and made me change the sheets.

"Don't put Georgina in bed with us".

I told Georgina to wait until Daddy fell asleep, and I slept with her in her little single bed. It was lovely, and we had many cuddles. I read her Peter Rabbit and Mrs. Tiggywinkle and watched her go to sleep. She was so beautiful, so peaceful, but I knew this couldn't go on and let her watch this abuse for much longer. We needed a plan to get out. An abusive relationship does not always start off as abusive. Usually, the victim is subjected to months of grooming. The perpetrator will often see the signs of vulnerability, offer protectiveness, shower them with possessions they may not have, or offer financial stability. They build your self-esteem; you think you can trust them with anything and they are the most wonderful person on the earth. Then they let you down once and then, piece by piece, pick away at your vulnerabilities, leaving you isolated, ashamed of what you have become, but unable to remove yourself from the abuse.

With Jimmy, I was looking for something that appeared missing from me. I felt that I did not fit into my family; he was a handsome man who could fight and was so strong. People were frightened of him, so my naivety led to him protecting me.

Jimmy said that his mother died, and he saw her dying. He was then brought up in a care home, and then, as a young boy, his father was asked to take care of him and his siblings. His father had remarried, so now Jimmy had a stepmother, who at first showered him and his siblings with gifts and love. She promised never to hurt them and to be their mum. His father was a drunk and believed that a woman obeys her husband. He used to work and then returned home very drunk and attacked her.

She had given birth to three other children and now had his three children to look after. She was made to keep the house immaculate. She was a beautiful blonde woman, a bit of a Marilyn look-alike in her younger days before she met his father; by the time she married him and had taken on his kids, she had let herself go, put on weight, and became extremely bitter. She was from the old-school generation; she was not going to leave him, but unfortunately for Jimmy and his siblings, her bitterness turned to physical and emotional violence.

Jimmy said that his father took to drink, when his mother left him. He felt humiliated, and people in the family said she was the only woman he ever loved. Nobody spoke about her life with him and why she left, but she died anyway at a very young age. She was a tall woman with a stunning figure and a very pretty face. However, a family member told me that Jimmy's dad was a jealous man with his second wife, and she was never allowed outside without him. At a very young age, Jimmy, as the eldest child, used to run errands for her.

Jimmy did not have a very good education, as he was made to stay home, clean, and run errands for his stepmother. His younger siblings were babies, and he was made to clean and look after them. He was often beaten if he did not clean properly, had black eyes, and frequent trips to the hospital, but nobody said anything in those days. They always said, "They are a tight family, and if you hurt one, you hurt each other."

For such a close family, I often used to ask why they did not put a stop to this. But then I was treated to a slap round the face, not too hard, but hard enough that it left a mark. He then said it was a reaction and did not mean it. I was putting him and his family down, which made him angry. He was also humiliated by wearing clothes as a child that did not fit him properly, so as an adult, he was always immaculate and desired designer clothing. He always smelt of a particular cologne, and I can't stand it now if I get a hint of a hit. It makes me nauseous.

I felt so sorry for him; I wanted to give him the family he wanted. All he wanted was love, and I understood that's why he was so happy for a virgin to be the mother of his children. Jimmy wanted someone to love him and have someone he could show off; he wanted a nice house and beautiful children. But life is complicated, and Jimmy could not see that he was punishing me for what happened in his childhood.

The control had started early in our relationship; losing my virginity was a traumatic experience. I was his woman now and belonged to him. Other boys were not allowed to talk to me in front of him; he would threaten them, and they would back off. He was frightening, but I felt flattered that this man was looking out for me, protecting me. I had a low opinion of men and was happy with this. In a way, I consented to the first method of control.

He was so tough as well. I saw him stand in front of a man waving a shooter at him.

He said, "Fucking do it, kill me then!"

This was over some money that was owed to a friend of his. It wasn't even his argument, but my brave Jimmy sorted it out. He took the gun off this bloke and hid it in a car before a member of his family removed it. I had held a gun and saw him avoid being shot. He was my absolute hero, not quite replacing Grandad, but he was the closest thing to it.

I had not been brought up with this life, but it was so exciting. He wanted to be with me and know where I was to protect me. He protected me from other men who tried to hurt me. The little punches and pinches I received when I saw and commented about a good-looking actor or band. Wearing his work boots (steel toe capped), he kicked me in the shins if his cousin dared to mention that I looked nice. I was told not to give him any attention and to stand behind him so he could not see me properly. The little bruises down my spine when I wouldn't show enthusiasm when he wanted to make love to me. These were all his ways of protecting me.

His idea of love-making was shoving his cock in me and cumming within a few seconds. There was no foreplay, and I don't ever remember him kissing me in public as I stood behind him. I could not understand why my friends enjoyed sex so much; it hurt and made me stink. He never made sure I was turned on, so he often went in dry, and it felt for a few seconds my insides were being ripped. I was never considered, so I just lay there waiting for it to be over, hoping for a few seconds that the actions would lead to me having a child. It was worth the inconvenience, and I did not know any different.

11 | Dirty Old Bastard

We were about five years into our relationship, so by this time, I was at times conforming to his rules; I had lost my babies and had my precious Georgina. I felt we would not be having any more children together. He was still abusing me; the new trick was humiliation and the fact I could not take him in certain positions, especially doggy.

After watching porn in earlier years I retained the information and experience - not for him but for my own benefit. I would never have anyone else insult me for how I was in the bedroom. I never climaxed with him, but if I gave him a few moans, the thick cunt was happy. He used to rape me as a form of control, he could not understand why I completely froze when I knew that it was coming. He did not believe in dildos as they took away his masculinity, so he had been told to freeze vegetables and use them as a way of opening me up. I was horrified and prayed to God that I would not be made to do this. Please, anyone, get me out of this one; I would even take a beating! The plan before this was a threesome, of course, another woman who would have been his friend's wife, and she would not touch me, but we would be pleasuring him, kneeling to him. I'm not sure he approached his friend's wife, but they were quite flirty towards each other at one time. However, she used to compliment me more than him and always touched me, saying how much she admired my clothes or lips, so I think she wanted me more. This was unacceptable to Jimmy, so he never mentioned it again. He did not know about Megan; he was the one who was abused as a child. He did not have a Mum, and he used to get beaten up, so I chuckled to myself that it must have hurt his ego that she rejected him for me.

He bought a cucumber and a carrot on this particular day and stuck them in the freezer. The stupid prick did not let them thaw when he tried to insert the carrot inside me. It stuck to my skin, making me more tense and unwilling to open. I got smacked round the face, and the carrot shoved into my mouth. I was made to hold it in my mouth while he fucked me. He threatened to stick the cucumber inside my arse. I was so tired of the threats and punishments; I begged if there was a god to free me. God did answer me, but he never freed me.

The following day, I was at my Mum's with Georgina; I was allowed to go out with my Mum or stay there during the day. A call came through that Jimmy was in hospital after some scaffolding had become loose, causing him to fall from roof height. He was going down to have an operation as he had mangled his foot and leg. He had landed feet first and, unfortunately for me then, not headfirst.

I left Georgina with Mum and rushed up to the hospital, and by the time I got there, he'd had his operation and was in the ward. Both his legs were up, and he had pins in them. He was on pain relief, so he knew I was there but was semi-conscious. He was a bastard while he was in the hospital; I had to visit twice a day and bring him fresh food as he would refuse to eat their shit. And if I brought Georgina up to see him, she would get bored, so it meant that I would leave him earlier than he wanted. So, Georgina was left at my Mum's, and I was told to sit with him all day. Jimmy was confined to a frame initially, but his specialist advised him that he would never walk properly, always be in pain, walk with a limp and would never do manual labour again. He was a selfish bastard; I was so relieved when he came home.

When he was discharged, he was so paranoid, and I was accused of poisoning him. He had difficulty moving, and with his personal hygiene, so I had to help him. I became a prisoner in my own home. After taking Georgina to school, I was questioned if I stopped at the shop. I would be accused of talking to the men on the market and shagging them. I would be told to bring him my underwear so he could sniff them, and if there was the slightest discharge, that would be interpreted as spunk.

Every day, this continued, and I could not take any more of his spiteful comments. So, I started to retaliate, as I could see he was weak. He couldn't catch me or get to me now. I left him in the bath for three hours with his leg hanging over the side, and I left him inside all day while I took Georgina out and saw one of my friends. He could not get to me. I left him at the hospital, and he had to get a cab back. I also hit him with his crutch, swiped a jumper across the pins on his legs and laughed while he cried out in pain. This was only temporary, though. The pins came off, and he walked with a limp, but now I was accessible once more.

Jimmy compared me to the woman in the film "Malice", but to me, I was getting my own back. His inability to be the breadwinner was a big deal to him as he got stronger and stronger. His ego had been flattened but we needed money quickly. Jimmy never wanted me to go to work; he wanted to be the breadwinner and earn the money. He also wanted me to stay at home so he could keep an eye on me to make sure I wasn't talking to any men or being, as he called it, a "fucking slag". But my girl needed new clothes, and we needed food to entertain our regular guests. I applied for a job and he wasn't happy when I got it, but reluctantly agreed as we needed the money. Also, I planned to work then to save enough to get away. With him always in the flat, it was hard to keep anything a secret. He would never leave me or Georgina; I would have to escape when the time was right. But when was the right time?

So work was finally my freedom for three hours a day. The office and kitchen were based in an industrial unit a couple of miles away. My job was to take hot meals to elderly people within a thirty-mile radius within two hours. I had half an hour to get there and half an hour to return. I made Jimmy lunch before I went and packed food for Georgina.

He still often spent time with Laura downstairs. She was a young single mum, my confidante and friend, someone I thought understood what I was going through. She did have a few boyfriends, and Jimmy felt she was a bad influence on me. He was so proud of me, as he was the only man I ever slept with. That was his ego talking, obviously, but when he was with me, and she came up, he insulted her by calling her a slag, throwing his crutches at her and telling her to get out. In his defence, she was shagging and after everything that moved. She was known as the local bike. But she was my friend, and she kept him company when I wasn't there. I trusted her and she used to tell me everything when I came back from work, so I thought!

Jimmy was a smoker, and in his younger years, he used to go to raves and take ecstasy and speed. It was the drink that made him violent. I hated it when he drank, as I used to get the worst of his rage. It did put a stop to him entering me and having sex, which was a good thing, but he was vile.

Laura was leaving her daughter asleep and coming up to us with a bottle of vodka or Jack Daniel's some nights. I used to say to her that Jimmy was still on medication, and this made his paranoia worse. She never used to listen and tell me to leave him if he was that bad. It was like she wanted to see me battered the next morning because alcohol had a negative effect. He would then say he did not want her coming up as she was a whore especially when she was the local bike. But every day at lunchtime, he took Georgina and went down to see her to have lunch. I was happy as Georgina had a playmate and another woman keeping an eye on her.

Jimmy always offered food to our regular guests (his mates), which could be at any hour of the evening. He never considered what I wanted or what was good for Georgina. He wanted his friends to come round, and so they did. I was there to make food and not back-chat him. If I did or made a sarky comment, I would pay for it later. It was like living on eggshells, but sometimes I thought I was going to get it anyway, so I'd think 'fuck it - let's play up'. He'd accuse me of constantly flirting with his friends; nobody was allowed in when he wasn't there, not even his family members: only my mum and a couple of my friends. Sometimes, he would be abusive to my friends if they shared their opinion about how unhappy he was making me. They saw the decline of a once happy person to someone frightened to talk to or comment on something he didn't like. When he was working, he instructed me to wear makeup for him to return home, but if the makeup were on when he was out, I would be in trouble.

Every day at work, I would deliver meals to customers. I may be the only person they saw that day, week, or anytime. However, I had time restraints; I had to deliver the food within two hours regardless of traffic. London is very busy and always congested. If I came back late, I had to deal with Jimmy, and I didn't want my customers to have cold meals, especially my favourites. Sometimes, my manager asked me to deliver to different routes as they recognised I knew London. He would then cover my customers, and I would take a new route. Try explaining that one to Jimmy! I didn't know the customers, so I was unfamiliar with keys, who would be in the house, where they wanted it and any other details.

One day, I was delivering and knocked at the door; a man answered it. He looked very dishevelled, and the house stunk of piss. There was an awful odour as I stepped in through the door, wishing and praying I would not have to undo the lid on his meal and get the cutlery from his kitchen. I noticed a woman lying in a bed, lifeless, not even acknowledging that I entered.

He said, "That's my wife."

I said, "Hello, I have brought you your dinner".

"Sorry, love, she won't eat it; that's for me. She has Alzheimer's; she can't talk or eat or anything. I am waiting for her to die."

Immediately, I heard that his tone was not said in sympathy or as a desperate carer.

"She was never pretty like you; will you be coming again?"

I then asked if she could hear what he was saying.

He then replied, "I don't think so; she wasn't pretty when she was well; in fact, she was fucking useless".

I felt so sorry for this woman, and although I wanted to react to his statement, my instinct told me to shut up. How did I know if he was the only one who cared for her?

"We've been married for over sixty years; useless cow couldn't even provide children for me".

I was boiling at this point. Would this woman be me in forty years? She had probably put up with his stench and abuse for years. Was death a release for her?

I was daydreaming when he suddenly grabbed my face and plonked a kiss on my lips from out of nowhere. Oh my god, the smell and the taste.

I immediately spat out on the carpet and wiped my lips, saying, "You dirty old bastard".

I ran out of the door, leaving the food on the sofa. I felt the roughness of the stubble from his chin and the stench of bacteria from his dentures that slipped when he spoke. I could not get the stench off my lips but knew I had a couple of dinners left on my list.

I had to return to the unit. One of the managers was there, and I told her what had happened. I was in total shock and had to use the tap to gargle and wash my mouth and lips. I could still smell the stench of the house and him. When I told her that under no circumstances would I visit there again, I got a bollocking for calling him a dirty old bastard. Now, I would have made a safeguarding referral as I was really concerned for the welfare of that poor woman. Still, at that time, I was so angry that another man thought it was his right to touch me. Also, I was very late and knew I would get the silent treatment for a couple of hours or be called a dirty slag. Or even if he was in a bad mood, or I told him about the incident, then I'd get hit and told that I encouraged it. It would mean no more jobs or money to buy Georgina toys and nice clothes. Or save up for our way out. I dreaded going back that day, traumatised about what had happened but terrified of what was coming.

12 | Distractions

Generally, everyone at work was nice. A couple of times on a Sunday, the person cooking did not correctly count the number of meals, meaning a blind lady would not get her dinner. As it was near my Mum's, I asked her to put some roast dinner in a box. I could not bear anyone to go hungry or miss a call. I knew some drivers wouldn't bother about the most vulnerable who could not inform the office that they had not received their meal. I would cut up their dinner and spend a few minutes trying to share some sunshine with them. Inside, I was miserable knowing that every few minutes spent chatting would result in a punishment for me.

The business was based on an industrial site, so there would be men working; I wouldn't dare lift my head and acknowledge the wolf whistles as if it went back to him, I would have to give up the job, and my baby would miss out on the extras.

The chef was lovely, and I instantly was drawn to her personality and humour. She was Turkish and knew a couple of the men working in the next units.

She used to say to me, "Man, if I had your fucking looks, I wouldn't be working here. You stupid cow, do you realise the effect you have on men? Ali next door calls you his ten and is obsessed with you."

I used to laugh and tell her she was crazy.

"Do you not see the way men look at you? They fucking drool".

She used to make me laugh with how she spoke in her broken Turkish-English dialect.

"Go and meet some rich Arab and he will spoil you and take you away from this shitty job. I know someone for whom that is working; you don't have to sleep with these people, but you won't get the goods."

I used to say, "I am not a prostitute; what are you going on about?"

One summer day, I decided to wear a pair of cut-downs, a vest and boots to work. Jimmy was downstairs with the neighbour; otherwise, I would not have been able to go out like that. I sneaked down the stairs and got in the car. I saw a twitch in the nets and automatically knew I would be in trouble for not saying goodbye. He made me feel so shit that morning and kept calling me ugly and fat, so sod it!

It was hot in the car and even hotter, taking out the hot food from the hot box in the boot of my car. I never wore make-up for work and tied my hair in a long plait for hygienic purposes.

I entered the kitchen, and Maria said, "Wow, look at those legs. Has Ali seen you?"

I immediately laughed at her comments and loaded the car. When I returned the hotbox to the unit, I saw Ali looking out from the doorway. I went straight home as I was already late and knew I would be in trouble and get additional shit for showing my legs.

The next day, I was recovering and sore. Jimmy had hit my legs with his stick and caught my back, too. He was always kicking me in the hips, and the bruises would turn yellow and disappear, so I went back to wearing jeans. He said sorry and then tried to say I went about looking like a slag and could not give him sex. During this time, the injury was a perfect excuse not to sleep with him, but it didn't stop him from further punches in my lower back and kicks to the hip. Georgina never liked her room, and it was the perfect excuse to cuddle her in bed and take the punishment, making sure she never felt it. I stopped the tears after a while and began to accept the pain as I had learnt to do.

While I was working, another incident involved my friend Maria, who was friends with Ali's wife. She said that after work, Ali came straight in, pulled her knickers to one side and bent her over. She said he fucked her like he had not had sex for years.

Maria asked, "Do you realise that was because you wore those shorts?"

She thought it was funny, but I felt guilty for his wife. Maybe Jimmy was right; if he had known of Ali's thoughts, the unit would have been trashed and burnt, with him probably in it. I would be black and blue because, of course, it was my fault. I caused that. Maria was concerned about why I wasn't laughing.

"That was the best fuck she's had in years; she felt wanted."

Either way, I couldn't win; it was my fault, anyway you looked at it. Why was I looked at like a piece of meat and not genuinely liked or respected for being myself, a young woman trying to earn some money.

13 | Escape

The violence was getting worse; it was happening every day. I was getting punched and kicked in the legs or the hips for not fulfilling my duties as a so-called wife and mother. Jimmy would check the flat daily to see if there was any dirt, as he called it. He was at home all day as he would never be going back to work due to the accident. He was smoking and drinking more. Every day, I felt I was shrinking more and more, becoming less of the person I had once been. I felt crushed inside and out and knew that if I didn't escape, then I would die.

Our last Christmas was unpleasant. I continued to work, clean and entertain the many guests. Jimmy's behaviour was becoming more extreme, and he was happy to shout and push me around in front of them. Nobody said anything to Jimmy as they were also frightened of his temper. They tried to look sympathetically at me if they were not within his stare.

If the children of the friends made a mess, he would say in front of them, "She needs to clean this fucking mess; she's a lazy cunt."

When I implied that I was the only one working in the household, he would get up and then get in my face.

"I said clean that fucking mess."

He would ask his friends how many times they had sex as "this stupid cunt couldn't or wouldn't do it; she couldn't even keep a baby without losing it".

I started to retaliate out of desperation. I threw a coaster at his head, which dented the wall as I was so drained of his comments. Obviously, I suffered for that. I said that I was going to leave him when I could, but that to an abuser is the worst statement as it makes them more paranoid. If I went to the shopping centre, he would set a time for me to return, and if I was late, I would get it regardless of who was visiting.

Jimmy was clearly suffering from the injuries following his accident. Still, mentally, it felt like he was switching from an angry man to a dangerous man. It was the first of January when I said that I'd had enough and went to bed, dreading his hands on me. I felt that even when he tried to be nice, he was inflicting pain. He was still up and smoking with his friends, and Georgina was in bed with me.

I woke up to the sounds of "Look what you made me do cunt".

I looked across and saw his wrists bleeding.

"If you leave me, then I am going to kill myself".

The cuts were not deep enough to do the job, but I got out of bed and cleaned them up.

For the next six months, I was subjected to his threats of pouring acid on my face so no one would fancy me, and I couldn't leave. Or he was going to burn me to ashes, then they would not find my body. This really scared me; my Georgina would only have him, that mad, crippled, dangerous man. He would come up to my face and make horrific threats, pressing my nose or slamming me against the mirrors to demonstrate who would want someone like me with a huge cunt. I was no good to Georgina and couldn't even give him more children. I was becoming more and more withdrawn, and the only person I really saw was my neighbour, who was always encouraging me to leave him and sympathising with his behaviour.

"He's going to kill you," she'd declare.

Georgina had started school, and I did not want to disrupt her, but it appeared that she was now noticing what was going on at home. She continued to sleep with me, saying she was scared in her room. But Jimmy objected to it. He would slam objects in the middle of the night, waking us up, or sometimes, he would continue to flick the light switch on and off. I would hold her close and tell her to go back to sleep; no one would hurt her - but this abuse was hurting her, and I needed to get out. I had contacted the Police to record an incident but refused to press charges. I needed an account so that if he did kill me, Georgina would not go with him but to my mums.

The night before I left, he put a pillow over my face, and I nearly stopped breathing. Georgina was in our bed but, fortunately, never woke up. Tomorrow, I was leaving; I knew he was going out; a friend was taking him out, so I had time.

I told three people I was leaving, as I had to be careful. It was Laura downstairs, one of his friend's wives, Rachel, who was also subjected to abuse. Her alcoholic, woman-driven husband used to ignore her most of the time. Still, she was unsure which was worse: a man waving his accomplishments of love bites and the residue of lipstick stains on collars or Jimmy. Even so, she was the one who encouraged the cousin to take Jimmy out. Laura, my friend, helped me pack. She wrote down all the contacts I would need on a piece of paper, and I left with my most personal documents, my prized possessions of photos of Georgina; I did not leave him with one photo. Six bags of clothes and toys, and that was it. I left my beautiful home and ran.

I did not have a clue about refuges and helplines for domestic abuse. I ran to my Mum's, and we lived in the attic bedroom until we were placed in a safe house. I went to the Police and told them I was leaving him due to his last attack. My Mum made all the arrangements and was constantly on the phone to the council as she knew he could get us at any time. I did not have a mobile, so the only access was the house phone. Anytime we felt he could get us, we went to the attic room as it may give us time to get the Police.

Laura, my friend, gave me the biggest opportunity to get away, although, at the time, I was so betrayed and hurt by Jimmy. Two weeks later after leaving Jimmy, Laura wanted to know if I minded if she had Jimmy. I couldn't believe my ears, the times I had confided in her, and she encouraged me to leave.

With a broken heart, in complete despair, I said, "Go for it and see what he does to you."

I cried in my Mum's arms as I could not believe what I had heard. She helped me escape, but she was now his distraction, so it gave me time to move twenty miles away to a bedroom with Georgina.

The room they gave us was stupidly closer to Jimmy than my Mum's security. It wasn't secure; it was an old, privately rented house that held two other women. This was supposed to be safe, but these women used to enter the room and have friends over throughout the night. During the day, I would drop off Georgina while I worked and then would return to the room after dinner at my Mum's. My Mum was constantly on the phone trying to get me nearer because if he or his family found out where I was, he would come and get me. When the door lock was tampered with, she kicked off and got me the house down her road.

We managed to get a solicitor to start the court proceedings and changed Georgina's last name to mine. He never turned up to court; he was handed the restrictions, but fortunately, his time now had been taken up by Laura's seduction techniques. I was a virgin before meeting Jimmy; my experience of sex was nil. I refused, unless forced, to have sex with him. Laura, however, was very experienced; she had already slept with his mate and had an affair with one of his family members, so she filled that gap. But she wasn't me, and she tried to become me during their time together. It tortured me for a year, thinking about them together in bed. Even though he subjected me to so much torture, he was the only person that I had been with, and although at the time I hated him for so many years, part of me loved him also. How the fuck was I going to move on? Leaving someone is not always as easy as people think; it opens a series of scars and wounds that never heal. I would never be the same person again. I had my daughter and my family; I lost friends, and my so-called best friends betrayed me. People think that after leaving, it's all done and dusted. They are so wrong.

When I left Jimmy, I allowed him to see Georgina until he could no longer protect her. He was either on drugs or drunk. He always fought with people, and many of his family disowned him. After leaving him I found out he had children with Laura and another woman, but never contributed towards any of his children. He also allowed Laura, my old friend, to emotionally harm Georgina on an overnight visit. She was so jealous and insecure about me that she inflicted this by shouting down Georgina's ear, "I hate your mum". Georgina came home from this visit very emotional and, after experiencing a nightmare, told me what had happened. I immediately called Jimmy and advised him that my mum would visit him with Georgina to prove she was telling the truth. Obviously, the girlfriend denied it, and Jimmy did not believe Georgina. He could not protect his child, so she could not visit. She was torn from the love of her father but scared after the incident.

Before the incident, every Sunday evening, Georgina would take a couple of days to get out of not talking to me. Jimmy and his girlfriend would insult me, leaving Georgina totally confused. My mum pleaded with Jimmy, stating he was living with a perpetrator who had done this to his daughter. He never believed it; after everything he said about his childhood, he believed the woman instead of his child.

It starts with a smile and butterflies
The warmth of a kiss
That loved one, every minute you miss
The same lips that tell you the lies.
The touch and caress every night in bed
The perfumes and creams
The soft whispers in the ears
It's not what it appears
For what you perceive
Is now dead.
So, it may seem uncouth
As you long for the truth,
Now, existing in hell
Wishing in heaven above
Imagination or naivety
Were you ever loved?

14 | The American Diner

Sharon was one of my best friends. Her brother said a job was going at a diner in Bruce Grove in Tottenham, in one of the back streets. He said the manager needed a waitress, and I needed the money as I just moved into the new house. I continued working as a delivery driver for the Meals on Wheels service but needed more money for Georgina.

Our house was a privately rented accommodation; the floorboards were creaky, and the old furniture and everything was so bleak. Before we lived there, it was a brothel. Yep, opposite a church in a respectable neighbourhood. We tried to clean up the garden and found drug paraphilia and condoms, but at least I was safe away from Jimmy. If he ever tried to get me, Georgina could run to my Mum's, and whatever happened to me, she wouldn't know about it. I never considered if it mattered to her if he killed me and how she would be without her Mum. She had her Nan, who loved her and would look after her. It never occurred to me that I also was a daughter to my Mum. Not sure about my Dad, he was always pissed and down the pub. When I think about what I put my Mum through, I just never thought about me and my safety.

In abusive relationships, you are living on the edge and existing; if you reflect on everything that is happening to you, then you would finish it yourself. My five-year-old daughter was the only person in the world who kept me going. Her happiness was my world, so I provided her with everything she wanted.

I was successful in getting the job. I had to wear a long black slinky dress, and my long hair plaited down my back. I wore heels and makeup. The other waitresses were polished and wore the traditional black and white uniform. They held six plates of food, where I could only hold two, but I could shake my arse when walking up and down in between the tables. I shared the tips with other waitresses, and we earned well until the manager decided he would take a cut.

Yes, I was a shit waitress, but I was good to look at, taking orders, and meeting and greeting the customers. Some regulars wanted liquor and coffee at the end of the shift at two in the morning. One specific customer would ask me to unplait my hair and shake it out. But he would pay a good tip, and shaking my hair is not exactly a crime.

I was getting a little pissed off with a table of men one night; listen, I don't mind the odd compliment, but one of them was getting a little crude and suggested that I should do some lap dancing, and he knew a friend who would welcome me. He then said I could make five times more in a night. In this job, I was covered, wearing a dress, shaking my hair and wiggling, whereas showing flesh was an entirely different issue. If I wanted to make money, then I certainly wasn't doing that. I tried to ignore his comments and talked to other customers when he tried to grab my arse to get my attention. Unfortunately, he had not been served any food before this.

The bell rang for table twenty, "I'll get this", I said and then walked over, swinging my hips, smiled, and accidentally let his meal fall onto his lap.

It was hot, so it would have burnt his crotch.

"Oh, I am so sorry", his friends laughed, knowing exactly what had happened.

Feeling humiliated, he went to the toilet, wiping the mess off him while the manager pathetically apologised. He knew what had happened, and I wondered if it was the end of my new profession. I received a bollocking; it never occurred to him that a customer groped me. So, I was in a bad mood then, and there would be no hair shaking tonight, fuck the tip.

In the corner was a weird professor lookalike; as he poured over his menu, he pointed at me to take the order. He was very elaborate, pointing at what he wanted on the menu. His glasses were perched on the tip of his nose, and I watched his thin lips articulately pronounce what he wanted. God, he was annoying; he kept stalling me there, and I was still pissed off at the previous customer, who proceeded to keep giving me daggers at the other side of the diner.

I gave the weirdo his food and knew he was perving over me. I could feel his eyes on my arse, and it felt really uncomfortable; it was not a normal glance; he was taking off my clothes, looking me up and down. I was completely out of control; the manager would not say anything, and I hoped he would not stay long. It was already late, but no, he called me over again.

I asked, "Would you like to see the dessert menu?"

He paused and then quietly said something I didn't quite hear.

He then moved his face to my ear and whispered, "Cunnilingus".

That was it; I cracked him one on the nose, and my days as a waitress were over. I tried to defend myself, and I got sacked. He never pressed charges, but I needed a new job.

15 | The Proposal

Although I'd left Jimmy, I was still best friends with Isabella, his uncle's wife. She helped us throughout my relationship with Jimmy. Now, these were times before all the tax credits and help with benefits, and apart from earning a small amount from Meals on Wheels, I had no money. I did not want to keep sponging off my family, so I chatted to her about trying to get extra money. I had previously sold some trainers and a few bits from the back of a lorry.

Isabella had a large family and, at times, would look after Georgina for me. Her family were lovely, apart from her brother Jack. He was also a good friend to Jimmy; nobody knew exactly what he did for a living, but they always had plenty of money. It was well known he used to visit brothels and sell dodgy knocked-off watches. Isabella said his wife, at the time, complained he was sex mad and was always up for it, so who knows? It would be the last place I would want my man to go and visit to sell watches. I wasn't the best person to give advice.

My best friend was so generous; she knew I was struggling and never went out, only to work. Sometimes, she would buy concert tickets, saying I needed to smile. She bought me tickets to see Take That and always bought Georgina gifts. She was a good friend, but it was difficult for her to be friends with me when Jimmy was bringing his new girlfriend to visit them. He was subject to a restraining order due to the violence, plus the fact Isabella felt uncomfortable talking to her.

Jack knew of my predicament because I was so skint, so he asked me if I was interested in a new business venture. He said he had a mate who was looking for a receptionist. So, we arranged to meet. Isabella came with me, and we met in a pub. Jack was there with his friend Lee. Lee appeared to be a vain man around his late forties, his hair in a style appropriate for a much younger man; it was obvious he was wearing foundation to cover his bad skin. He made my skin crawl. He was so slimy - looking at every young girl in the pub. Lee said he had a small business coming up and wanted me to be the receptionist. I would get £70 a day to answer the phone, but I needed a certificate with my name above the door, a kind of registration. It didn't occur to me what was coming next; I thought it was a new shop selling his watches; never in my wildest dreams did I think he would come up with this plan.

Lee said, "Listen, it will be a place where lots of girls will be inside; all you must do is answer the phone and press the buzzer."

Isabella asked, "Hang on, are we talking about a brothel?"

Lee replied, "Yep, you guessed it, but you need to go and do a massage course and register it in your name."

I was speechless.

Isabella asked, "For what? When is it your business? What the fuck are you going on about?"

"Come on, let's go, it sounds proper dodgy, Ju."

Lee said, "Don't go. No, honestly, you will earn that money for answering the phone and pressing the buzzer. Please do not think I am discriminating against sex workers, as we all must earn a living."

I had only slept with Jimmy, and the last thing I wanted me to think about was having sex or booking sex.

I was getting on so well with my mum; I told her everything, including this plan, but she obviously was against it. She did not want me to do it, but I had left everything with Jimmy; I would eventually need to make a home; I was only just making ends meet. I would only have to work two days, which would be it, but I would get more money and more time for Georgina. I was vulnerable and too naïve to think any different.

Jimmy went mad when he finally found out about this proposal; he did not want the mother of his daughter working in a brothel like 'one of them'. We never got anything from him, but his duty was to protect his reputation.

Another friend of mine also advised me that it would be my body they would want and that I could get killed in one of these places, hurt, attacked or even raped. (They didn't know anything about me). So I decided the next time I was contacted, I would tell Jack to inform Lee I wouldn't be working for him.

When Lee rang, he told me the massage course was coming up, and I needed to do it.

I said, "Nah, Lee, thanks, but I'll give it a miss."

Lee said, "If you give me a blow job, then you won't have to be skint."

I was absolutely disgusted and put the phone down. I cried to think that someone was going to try and put me through that after all I had been through. He was a prized prick!

I cried that night thinking about Lee's offer of a job and never-ending blow jobs. I called Jack and told him about Lee's proposal. Jack shouted at me down the phone, saying I was ungrateful and he couldn't see a problem. He would make a lot of money from me, and Lee had already arranged a list of clients.

He then laughed and said, "You can always fuck me; I have always fancied fucking you."

My head was spinning; how could I tell this to Isabella? So, I did the right thing; I arranged a last-time visit to my best friend and lied and said I would leave her for a while as she was related to Jack, and I couldn't be in the same room as him, blah blah. Isabella was hurt.

Her last words were, "You are incapable of loving a man, and you will never love or trust again".

I cried again that night and have never seen her since.

16 | Propositioned

It was time to move on again, as the council had just offered me a ground-floor, two-bedroom flat on a notorious estate. I didn't care as Georgina was near enough to her school. I was working for myself in a little cleaning business and selling Anne Summers at night. So, I worked through the day, dropped off Georgina to my Mum's and then went out with my kit full of dildos and naughty underwear to sell to women, who mainly squeezed into the skimpy items, played games and spread the cream onto the dildo. The winner of that game would see how deep-throat she could get the dildo. After it was over, I would clean them and put them away for another day. I became one of the highest sellers of dildos in the East region. I had dildos that would talk, tongues that vibrated and the rabbit with the extra bit for the clit. I had games, including packs of playing cards illustrating certain sex positions. As each party night went on, the women would try on the underwear and secretly order their merchandise. I would deliver and collect the money from the host a week or two later.

My cleaning company was mainly based in Northwest London. I cleaned for wealthy families - you name it, I cleaned it. So, we were never short of money. Jimmy still refused to pay maintenance and was living with his girlfriend Laura, who was now expecting his child. I'd left all my furniture in her flat. But it didn't matter; Georgina could have anything she wanted. However, I couldn't provide a decent father.

I purchased a bright yellow van to put my cleaning equipment in and washed the cloths every night to ensure they were ready for the next day. I was happy for a while.

My mum helped me decorate the flat, and we had everything we needed. The flat, we believe, was haunted, as the previous tenant had hung himself on my wardrobe door. But after a while, strange occurrences like music being turned off for no reason and items moving stopped. There was a courtyard and a small garden where Georgina played. I also cleaned for my next-door neighbour, an elderly woman across the road, to pay for Georgina's tutor once a week to help her with her reading. The teachers said she had dyslexia, but we managed to get her to a reasonable standard, so she was never behind in her lessons.

The courtyard was full of kids, often in and out of the flat. I used to feed them all, and Georgina had plenty of sleepovers. I was knackered and managed to go out a few times on dates, but it wasn't a priority. Because I worked and Mum had Georgina, it was hard to find a babysitter, and men were not allowed to come back to the flat. Although I dated, my opinion of men remained guarded due to Jimmy and, as I said, the attitude of men who thought they could buy me for sex because I was a single parent and cleaned for their family. Did I have a magnet or sign on my face or body to be treated like shit? Did I attract or do something wrong for these men to do this to me?

The first time it happened, I was cleaning a family home in a well-known Jewish community. This was only temporary whilst their regular cleaner was away. I was recommended by another family. While I was cleaning upstairs, the husband asked, while his wife was downstairs, if I could clean the house for him naked. I was absolutely flabbergasted; his wife was chatting to the children in the kitchen.

"Hang on, did I hear you correctly? Is this with your wife or without her?"

"Oh no, just me in the house. I would love to see you clean without any clothes on."

I replied. "How about you pay me now, and then you can tell your wife about your suggestion?"

He looked shocked!

"Also, you can tell her why I am walking out this door now and not coming back, and if you dare to spread any vicious lies about me, I will come back myself and tell the whole community I clean for."

I do not know what excuse he made, but no amount of money would bring me back to clean for them.

There are a few other examples of when this happened. Another Jewish husband asked me why I grabbed the broom like I was holding a phallus. My reply was for him to get out of the room, or the phallic shape would be shoved into something, and once again, I removed myself from the home. These people were professionals and supposedly honourable members of the community. Still, the husbands believed they could buy or suggest inappropriate sexual acts.

I cleaned for a family whose husband begged me to be his mistress and said he would take me to Marbella and leave expensive designer underwear and swimwear for me. His wife was an adorable English woman; she understood how hard it was to provide money as she'd been a single parent before meeting him. When she was in the house, he literally popped in, but there were times when I expected her, and it was just him. He never touched me; he just commented and left the underwear in my bag as an extra bonus. I never kept it but put it on eBay to sell. He said she knew about a mistress he had in France that he would pop over to see, and for at least two months of the year, he would go there for a holiday. In the end, I found out he died. I didn't have the heart to tell her about the extra bonuses, and I am sure I wasn't the only one he spent money on.

There was another husband who used to follow me around his house. His wife, who was disabled, would say to leave me alone and let me clean. He was over sixty, just a dirty old man unsure of what he wanted. He commented about me bending over even though she was in the room. What could I do? I couldn't afford to keep letting these jobs go. I just ignored him and offered an insult, which made his wife laugh. Maybe it was her way of getting him back for what she described as him being "cheeky".

A proposition came from a man who became my client. He was over eighty, very hairy and a typical little Jewish man in the diamond trade. He offered me diamonds for me to be his girlfriend. He was single, as his wife had died years ago.

He said he did not have any children. I could have milked him for a lot of money if I would have been that type of woman. I didn't know if he wanted just company or a younger woman on his arm. In a way, I felt sorry for him as he was old and probably lonely but he disgusted me at the same time. All I was doing was trying to make an honest living for Georgina and me.

It reminded me of when I worked for a cleaning company before I'd obtained my little cleaning business but had left the Meals on Wheels service. The boss was a slim Nigerian man; he had about a dozen women working for him, but he liked my spirit and possibly my looks. He used to give me all the good jobs, so after a while, I gave the clients a discount on price and cleaned for them. They were my regulars and were decent people. He used to charge them extortionate rates and pay us little. He eventually sussed out that I was poaching the jobs and asked me if I was doing it cheaper. I was honest with him.

He said, "You are very cheeky, but if you go now, that is the end of the matter."

It was a lucky escape, I guess! As I said, I had grown ruthless, but not enough to sell my soul. This is not intended to put down sex workers. I greatly admire personal choice; if it works for them, fine... exploitation is different. Abuse is exploitation.

17 | Gus

My dating days continued, and I met Gus in a London nightclub; he was with a group of friends: larger than life, taking the piss out of people and thinking he was a player. In hindsight, he was probably on coke and pissed.

I met a girl called Lauren that night; she was beautiful and had a great figure. I was totally in awe of her. She was alone drinking in the pub, and I started chatting to her at the bar and invited her to our group. Everyone was tired that night, but I wanted to go out and make a night of it. Nobody else except Lauren was up for it, and she suggested a club. Georgina was staying overnight at a friend's, so why not?

We arrived at the club and went to the bar, and I felt someone was looking over. Suddenly, a tall guy came over and asked if I could help him as he had something up his nose. It seemed such a bizarre thing to say, but I found it amusing. We started talking, and he asked me out. He told me he was a father to a two-year-old daughter that he adored and said he had her every weekend. I left early that night and left him in the club. (Many years later, he said he also tried to chat up Lauren but decided to call me. Prick! I didn't know that, so I went on a date with him.)

He gave me the whole sob story about his daughter and how his ex was a total bitch to him. He said he loved George Michael, and I was an absolute fan of him. He was also funny, so I liked him. That was a big mistake. I saw him often over the next few weeks and slept with him once. I became pregnant and found out on Georgina's' birthday. He was not at all supportive, demanded I get an abortion, and insisted that the baby wasn't his. I could not bring up another child on my own, so I did the unthinkable after losing so many babies, and I had an abortion.

My mum came with me that day and stayed with me, waiting while I had the procedure. Gus even had the cheek to borrow my car and brought it back in the evening. He did not show any compassion, and a week later, I was warned by an associate to stay away from him; he was a wanker.

I found out years later, that very day, he fucked a girl in my car, so he said anyway. So, he was more than a wanker. I think the name cunt is too good for him, but he was so alluring with his persistence when I never answered his calls. I saw him socially on and off for a year; I don't know why, maybe because, at times, he was fun to be with; did I deserve anyone really nice? Unfortunately, he was a known drug taker, and his ex-partner contacted me, claiming he was still in love with her. He said she was mad, and this was her way to get me away from him. I was seeing other people when he wasn't about; we had a no-sex rule, and only dating was allowed. It was my way to get back at men as I thought I was in control.

Gus offered Georgina and his daughter a holiday; I paid for our share but thought it would be nice for Georgina to get away. Only when we were on holiday did he show his true colours. I was not allowed to talk to people; he threw bouncy balls at me when I was naked and getting changed one night and threatened to burn my face with the iron he held so closely I could feel the heat. I wanted to go home, but Georgina was having her first holiday abroad, so I just went along with it, thinking I was going to get the fuck away from him when I got back.

He took my money, placed it in the safe, and then refused to return it. Georgina had been given some spending money to buy snacks and gifts for my Mum and Dad. I would often go out for early morning walks with Georgina, and Gus would be sleeping with his daughter. Before our walk, the usual routine was to rush down to the poolside, place four towels on the sunbeds and then go for breakfast. Gus would come down around ten, insinuate I was flirting, demand I go with his daughter Amy to get some food, and then he would order a beer. Georgina would be in the pool, making new friends. Amy, around four years old, would lie on her sunbed watching her father drink beer after beer. His mood deteriorated after every glass. I wasn't allowed to move very far out of his sight. I was screaming inside, but I saw Georgina smile; she was all that mattered. And I was planning another escape.

Gus was different to Jimmy. I did finish with him after the holiday, but he was very persistent; he would harass me, call me all night, and just turn up pissed or on coke; he broke my window once and just would not go away. Sometimes, he would turn up with Amy for the weekend after her mother would drop her off at Gus's every Friday and pick her up on Sunday evening. Gus would make an excuse that Amy was missing me and Georgina. Every weekend, he would take Amy to the pub until he was so pissed he could barely stand or talk. He made me feel guilty; the whole situation made me feel guilty, so often I let them stay. But it caused more problems, and I was unable to change the situation. How could I leave Amy with him?

Sometimes, I refused, but then I was challenged about how I could leave Amy when she loved me more than her mother. This caused an argument and, at times, resentment; I was looking after Georgina without a break; why would I take on an extra child when she had her own mother and father? It was a pleasure when Amy was with me; she was safe and happy. But it wasn't my responsibility; Amy had her own family. If I approached Gus with this, he used to call me a bad mother, call me names and be even more of a bully. He would hold a glass up to my throat or threaten to kill himself. There have been times when I called the police to remove him from my premises. But like a boomerang, he came back.

Gus's ex turned up with her new boyfriend one weekend and started arguing and fighting with Gus. The bloke had a baseball bat; stupidly, I got in between them and told them both to fuck off. The boyfriend landed Gus with a punch, and Gus actually shit himself; it was running down his leg when he ran out crying, "You've taken my daughter!" Unfortunately, Georgina saw him running out of the flat with shit literally showing through his shorts and oozing down his leg. She had the last laugh and, as a teenager, reminded him that he was a bully and could only fight women as men caused him to shit himself.

Georgina hated Gus with a passion. He always commented about Jimmy and how he was a shit father and that he couldn't be bothered with her. He then apologised to her, saying he would never do it again as I never allowed him to get away with these comments. It would cause another row, the police may be called, or he would leave, shouting obscenities and return later pissed or drugged up. Also, I refused to have Amy by this time, so she would be with him or his parents. This went down like a lead balloon, as they also didn't want Amy all weekend.

Gus was a coward who knew a few people from London whose parents were a little handy, so they basically lived off their parent's reputation. A gun was offered to him to shoot his ex-partner's boyfriend. He called me the day after the shit incident, but I persuaded him not to use it, but he sounded a mess and begged me to come round. I ended up sleeping with Gus out of pure pity. I took the morning-after pill within seventy-two hours as I knew I was extremely fertile. I wanted to get rid of him and everything associated with him.

That one occasion led me to get pregnant, and I found out I was three months gone with Roma when I went to the GP and was tested. I'd only slept with that pig twice after the incident with his daughter and ex. I would never get rid of another baby, so I knew I was lumbered with him. He was pleased that I was pregnant and wanted to make a go of our relationship. He even convinced me to get a joint bank account with him, and within three months of having an overdraft limit, he spent every penny, leaving me with the debt. It was extremely bad timing. I had just started a new job I loved, working in a mental health unit and continuing with my cleaning. I was not entitled to any additional benefits, so I just worked and started studying once a week at college. This was the start of me re-educating myself.

It was hard and tiring, and Gus never gave me a moment of peace. He insisted that his daughter stayed with us every weekend; if I said no and was not up to it, the guilt trip would ascend. Georgina was happy with her friends, but often, she said she was miserable as she knew how stressed I was. She knew that I would be expected to parent Amy nearly every weekend, and she was hard work. At age three, Amy had a dummy and blanket and ate baby food. Gus continued expecting me to take her out while he went up to the pub and got drunk. I was pregnant and working, but Gus would insist I pick him up. He would then expect a large meal and then drink another three bottles of wine, slowly falling to sleep, farting and stinking my flat out.

I was in a dilemma: why did I stay with this man? Georgina did not see her Dad, and I wanted this child to have a father figure, even though he was an arsehole. Gus was emotionally draining, calling me names when he was drunk or he'd start crying, saying how life was so unfair. I did not want him or his daughter; she was not my responsibility, and I could not parent her. I found it embarrassing and truthfully resented her when I took her out as she was like a spoilt baby, but at the same time, I felt sorry for her. Georgina sometimes found her annoying as she had to share a bedroom with her. Gus completely turned my life upside down, and I was allowing it. Why? I felt torn towards my unborn child to at least have the love of a father when I knew I was unable to fulfil Jimmy's love for Georgina. Surely Gus would love my child, too? It was all such a mess.

When I was six months pregnant, Gus kicked me in the leg when I told him not to bring Amy for the weekend. I was exhausted; I was carrying two jobs, studying and trying to do my best for Georgina, so I went to my Mum's with Georgina to get away and allowed him and Amy to stay at mine. This was not going to be a regular thing, but I was so desperate for my unborn child to have a father. Wherever he went, the child went, mostly. If I felt guilty, then she would come with me, or she would have been left with a bunch of coke heads in the pub, and that was no way to bring up a child. Her mother did not appear to worry about her; she just dropped her off every Friday and picked her up Sunday night.

Gus had to go into hospital after getting blood poisoning from standing on a rusty nail. Gus's mother was old and did not want her granddaughter, and she told me that I should have her. His mother was also a bully and barely spoke positively about her own grandchild. She was a nuisance but also too old to have her all weekend. So, once again, I did not have a choice; I had to have Amy. It was so different from my Mum; she adored Georgina and supported me throughout my pregnancy.

Two weeks before I gave birth, I was diagnosed with Pre-Eclampsia, and this was dangerous for the baby and me. Gus still insisted we went to his friend's fortieth wedding party. My ankles were like elephants, and my head was throbbing. He took his daughter and could not give a shit about how I was feeling or the risk to his unborn child. At thirty-six weeks of pregnancy, I finished working. I'd still been cleaning and lugging a heavy hoover about. I was induced at the hospital, as the risk was worsening. After twenty-six hours, I gave birth to Roma. Throughout the birth, Gus was useless; he had bought a stash of Stella and constantly went out for a break. All he wanted to do was to wet the baby's head and get out of his nut.

I was in hospital for a few days due to my ever-increasing blood pressure, but Gus wanted me home. I begged the hospital to let me go home earlier, and he promised to look after me. I also wanted to see my Georgina. That bastard made me cook as soon as I got home and never helped. Amy stayed, too, and was so demanding because she was jealous of the new baby. He went out and left us. Georgina helped me with Roma because I felt faint every time I stood up. I was breastfeeding and stressed. My baby had a hint of jaundice, but she was like a beautiful little doll. Two weeks later, I had to return to work; he was putting pressure on me and would not give me any money. I was not entitled to additional benefits, so with a heavy heart, I put Roma with a childminder and a nursery.

I never went back to my cleaning company and relied on the money from the mental health work. Gus was a useless, big, fat slob. A ponce who drank too much and was always farting. I decided to finish with him when Roma was two weeks old. I became so ill during the first few months trying to work and look after two kids. I was also still studying at college because I wanted a better life. My manager at work encouraged me to keep strong.

When Roma was five months old, I discovered that Gus must have crept in one night and, while I was unconscious, impregnated me. I do not know to this day how it happened; I had a fever and was ill. Roma was being bottle-fed by this time and was sleeping through the night, so I took some tablets just to keep my temperature down. He must have been let in by Georgina. Was I ill? It must have happened once! I don't remember ever sleeping with him after he left. Of course, he never left me alone, always calling and leaving vile messages. Still, I don't know how I became pregnant with Jake. It must have been him; I hadn't slept with anyone; I was exhausted, and the last thing I wanted was another child to look after alone. Gus looked shocked and happy when I told him I was pregnant.

Here I was in a small two-bedroom flat with a young girl, a baby and pregnant. I just had to get on with it. Throughout this pregnancy, I worked and continued to study, and guess what? I passed every exam and completed every assignment because I wanted more for my children and would get it.

18 | Is It That Bad To Be a Spurs Fan?

Life went on, and somehow, I managed - I certainly had plenty of experience. We were having a lovely Sunday afternoon in our flat; Georgina had brought a friend round to sleep for the night, Roma was two and a half, and my Jake was a baby. We returned from my Mum's after having a lovely roast dinner. Dad had not been well; within the last couple of years, he had fallen over through his drinking and had to go and get dried out in the hospital. My Mum and Dad were going to be moving away from the regular haunts, pubs and betting shops that enticed my Dad to spend his working day and night there. If he stayed in London much longer, he would be dead. Instead, they were off to the countryside, with the clean air, but unfortunately for Mum, pubs and off-licenses would still sell him the drink.

I rarely drink due to my Dad, and especially after the beatings I took from Jimmy when he was drunk. We have seen my Dad hallucinating from the drink; he became severely disabled due to alcohol damaging his nerves. He would drink anything he could get his hands on. And we asked why when he had everything he needed at home. He did not come from a broken and unloving family. He had a beautiful wife and two children. My Dad was a man's man and loved football, any sport, and talking absolute bollocks in the pub. When asked, he preferred the company of men.

His addiction has controlled my Mum for over fifty years, and she became his carer - washing and doing everything for him. Mum has not had a life for over twenty years because, for some reason, she never left him when she probably should have. My Mum never had the support; she kept silent regarding her needs, and family always came first.

Gus was also an alcoholic and would polish off three bottles of wine a night. But he insisted he never had a problem despite drinking until he became unconscious. He was a right mess - snoring and farting on the sofa or if he made it to the bedroom. A vile smell came out of his skin, and he became fat and swollen; his behaviour was pure harassment after I kicked him out when Roma was two weeks old.

Most Sundays, Gus would pick up Roma and Jake and then take them to his mother's and then a football club for a few hours, then he would demand I come and collect them, or he would leave them there. He tried to kidnap Jake once and made me get on my knees in the street and beg for him to give him back to me. His mother then stood over me and said I was mad and pathetic.

Before picking them up, even though I asked him to remain on the doorstep, he would shut Roma and Jake in the lounge and tell them to play while he spoke to Mummy. He would then rape me, and I could not make a noise or defend myself as they would hear. If Georgina was about, then he would leave me alone, but how can you stop a teenager from spending overnight at a friend's house or dragging her out of bed, fearing how he would attack me in the kitchen.

After he raped me, he would tell me I was a dirty slag and then take the kids out to the car. I would sink to my knees after saying bye and telling them to have a nice time. He kept photos of me that he took when we were together; he would snap me when I was changing or getting out of the shower, focusing on my breasts and vagina, enlarging the photos, and then distorting them, knowing I already had body dysmorphia from anorexia. If I did not let him have them, he would send me the vile images at work and at home, threaten to send them to the school and put them on lampposts. He once held me down and raped me with a cucumber, laughing after saying what a dirty slag I was. I had to protect my children in the next room so they would not discover the truth. He once pushed me into the cupboard in the kitchen and abused me anally. He then laughed and said I was no longer a bum virgin.

Gus knew I did not have much money and refused to pay maintenance; at this point, he was only legally required to pay £5 per child as he was no longer lawfully working. He would pull out a wad of dough and say you can have it if you sleep with me. Despite having nothing and now in mortgage arrears, I never took this money, so then he would continue to threaten me if I never picked up the kids when he demanded so.

He would spit in my face and call me a slag. After Jimmy and the assault, his physical threats were nothing; I was exhausted, so I learned to not react without any emotion. He then upped his game and would say he had a contract on me, and the kids would go to him. I could never get away from him like I did with Jimmy until he lost his license due to drunk driving, and he blamed me for that. If the kids wanted to see Gus, I would have to drive them to see them and pick them up. The length of the visits was decided by Gus; if he knew I had something planned, then he would disrupt my time and demand I collect the kids immediately. And I would drop everything because I loved my kids more than I despised him.

On this Sunday afternoon, there was a knock at the door. Georgina opened it, and there stood a pissed Gluttony Gus.

"I have come to see my babies".

I was in a position where if I told him to fuck off, there would be a scene, and Georgina was having such a lovely day. If he came in, then within an hour, he would be asleep on the sofa, and then I could tell him to fuck off in the morning. There was no way he was getting in my bed again. I had Roma's and Jake's cots in that room, and Georgina and her friend had the bunk beds. So that fat delightful piece of shit came in. Georgina's friend wore a Spurs shirt, and the little ones played with their toys.

Only Roma was pleased to see him; Jake had never liked him; even as a baby, he was always a Mummy's boy. Gus loved his little Roma with her cheeky smile and curly hair, but he still never paid for her but gave it the bollocks. So, Gus gave Roma a little attention for a few minutes, asked for some food and then dozed off.

Now I don't know what happened, but as I walked into the lounge after feeding Jake, he said, "Who's the cunt in the yid shirt?"

I asked him what he said again, looking at the TV and wondering if football was on.

He then pointed to Georgina's friend and said, "That little cunt in the yids shirt".

Now, to call me that name, I accepted, but not to a little girl who happened to be our guest. She was eleven years old, and a forty-plus man called her a cunt for no other reason than wearing a football top.

I opened the door and told him to get out.

"Don't you ever call a child that name."

Gus got up and went to the door; suddenly, he dragged me onto the floor by my hair and literally dragged me into the bedroom. I knew instantly what would happen, but Gus was no Jimmy; I could fight him. When I got to my feet, I punched him straight in the mouth and went to tell Georgina to walk with her friend to her house; by this time, the friend was screaming. I told Georgina to shut the living room door, go to her friend's house and get the police. Roma was screaming as Georgina left her and shut the door.

I then felt a crack on the back of my head and felt no more. When I came around, I looked at what knocked me out; that prick couldn't hurt me; he had used his boot to break the wooden pole off my bed and hit me with it. I woke up to him laying into me, but I fought back to get to my babies, who by this time were screaming for me.

I felt so full of adrenaline that I did not feel the blood coming from my head, my mouth, or my eye. I was going to fucking kill this cunt. I was not taking this anymore. He was pissed, so he was unstable, so I managed to push him out of the way and head to the lounge. I was going to my babies, and if anyone tried to stop me, I would have done anything.

I heard the police outside. Gus was smashing up my bedroom. I went to pick up Jake, and by this time, Roma was calm and watching the Tweenies. I went to open the front door when Gus, who must have seen the police arriving, went to leave. My son was in my arms when he pulled his arm back and stuck his finger in my eye. I screamed but did not drop my son. I had never felt such excruciating pain before. He walked out the door with his hands up, declaring his innocence. He got nicked; they saw the state of my face and said they would be back the next day for a statement.

We all slept in one bed that night, all of us petrified, traumatised. The next day, I had to get photographed and write a statement. I had a broken tooth and bruises to my face and body, and he had just missed permanently blinding me. I had to go to work and walk about with a blood clot in my eye for what seemed like an eternity. My tooth was replaced by metal as a reminder of that night.

My boss, at the time, said that I needed to pursue this conviction and obviously protect my kids from him ever doing this to me again.

It did not stop him. Two weeks before Jake's birthday, the front door was open, and Gus was lurking; he just walked in and raped me again, then told me he would say to the police that I consented and begged him. He threatened that he would tell everyone in court what a slag I was. I was too frightened of this threat; how would I be taken seriously in court now. Nobody would listen to me despite my injuries. My eye remained partially bloodshot, I'd had dental work, including a root canal done, and scars were visible. His voice and words provided that ever-increasing embarrassment. I was ashamed; I was working towards a professional qualification, responsible for supporting others with domestic abuse and mental health problems. How could I appear this vulnerable?

One Sunday, some time later, he turned up to the house. I could smell the drink on him and refused to allow Roma and Jake to go with him. He then turned on me in the street, and the neighbours took Roma and Jake to their house and called the police. His daughter Amy was in the car, too, so she had to wait at the police station until someone picked her up. Of course, I got the blame. Before the police turned up, he went to hit me in the face.

I removed my glasses; tired of this, he had already nearly blinded me, and I said, "Fucking do it, but they are not going with you."

His next trick was to take me to court. He was entitled to legal aid whilst I was working and paid for some advice. I represented myself in court, and he had a barrister. The outcome was for him to have supervised access for two years. He was on a driving ban, so despite her hatred for me, his mother took him every other week to the supervised centre. This centre involved the children who were subjected to a room in a church hall ordered by the court. I got abused by his mother for doing that to her son, and she paid for a couple of holidays as they got older, but they had the choice to go and knew nothing about what he had put me through.

After two years, Gus used to turn up to see Jake play football. Still, the promises of taking him every week did not suit him and turning up smelling of the nights before alcohol embarrassed Jake. He did not want him to watch him play anymore. I obviously got the blame, and he then would call, threatening and calling me names. Roma and Jake heard these names once and chose to disown their father.

19 | Bexley Road

Bexley Road was my route to happiness. I thought everything was going to change as I moved away from Gus. I didn't do it the easy way; I could have approached the council, saying that I was fleeing domestic abuse. I had the court case, restraining order, and everything. But no, I had my pride; I wanted to own a house so the kids had something I could leave them if anything happened to me. I am a cat, and I have nine lives, so eventually, one bad hit from one of those bastards would get to me and kill me. Gus always promised he would take out a contract on me. I was a walking timebomb but never frightened of Gus's threats. He was a pisshead and sometimes had a nose full of snow.

Our new home was an old terraced house that smelt of pissy carpets and had 1970s décor, but it was mine. The money wasn't transferred from my solicitor to the agent on the day I was supposed to move. After six hours of my furniture stuck in the van, two toddlers, a teenager, a puppy and a kitten, I was told I couldn't enter my new house. The removal men were going to put my furniture out on the streets as they were thoroughly pissed off.

Graeme was my saviour; he charged me eighty pounds to transfer my furniture to my mum's garage and then, the next day, moved me into my house. I can't remember who gave me his name, but he was my knight in shining armour, and I promised him I would pay him back the favour. Graeme was married to a lovely wife and couldn't understand why I was single and doing this by myself, but he was old school and couldn't bear to see a woman in trouble. We also shared the same birthday.

So that night, we all slept on the floor at my Mum's, including the dog and kitten. I'm not sure if it was trauma, but I started to bleed from my eye during the night. I never slept anyway; I had a baby and a toddler, so between them and studying, I only had two hours of unbroken sleep. I was working in London, so it meant getting up early and dropping Roma and Jake off at the nursery for six in the morning. But it was so worth it; I was the owner of a property, away from Jimmy and Gus, on a new journey, and a happy chapter.

Bexley Road was a weird street. Some neighbours could not understand how a single woman with three kids had just bought a house. I had a car, and the kids always wore nice clothes. I ensured the garden looked like Toys R Us while the house waited for redecoration. I went about my own business, worked all day, all night, sometimes at weekends in a residential home and studied. Georgina always had friends over, so the house was buzzing and full. Music was always playing, there was dancing and so much noise. We had Halloween parties, Christmas parties, tea parties, fireworks nights and birthday parties. The kid's rooms were packed with toys. Georgina always walked about from head to foot in designer clothes - she was a flash little showoff and always wanted the best. Most importantly, we all smiled and were away from the danger.

Unfortunately, it turned out I moved away from London only to move near a misogynist and a sex worker. The sex worker, Leah, was fifty-plus. She had a husband and two sons. She worked from home whilst her sons were at school, and her husband was a delivery driver. He knew what she did for a living and in their bed. But during the ten or more years I lived there, she spread gossip to other neighbours that I was a sex worker. When Roma's rabbit ran under the fence, the next thing we saw was a wooden cross and a fresh grave. She burnt down the kid's inflatable Father Christmas and was always knocking on the door pissed or would catch you as you were going through the door. She was a bloody nuisance and always passing comments. Looking back, I am unsure if she was lonely; she wanted to be my friend but had many peculiar little habits. She had a front garden, which was immaculate with fake flowers, lights and candles. She also used to put her Christmas decorations up after Halloween. But she was weird; the decorations were not based on cute, cuddly Santa Claus or cheeky elves, but skulls with tinsel, bats and objects hanging around. She also had a life-size model of a haunted butler as she opened the door. It was alleged she painted the tree outside my house with white crosses; somebody saw her do it in the middle of the night. I would find shavings of vegetable peelings outside my front door, all immaculately cut into hundreds of pieces. Very weird behaviour!

When I found out about this rumour about me being a prostitute, I went to her house and asked, "Did you call me a prossie?"

Leah obviously denied it. I then reminded Leah that if I was on the game, then I wouldn't be fucking living next to her.

I unkindly said to her, "How much do you charge? Forty pounds for everything?"

She then tried to be civil, but I was very annoyed; who the hell was she to talk about me, so I lost it a little.

"Look at you, you are a fucking mess, and then look at me".

She then tried to say that I banged my kid's head on the concrete. This was too far; she would get a piece of my mind. Nobody accuses me of hurting my kids, and the hurt and the violence that I had been through made me see red. I went for her and told her husband that she was a dirty slag, spreading nasty rumours that I hurt my kids. I threatened to fucking cut her fanny off so she couldn't work. That night, he left her. I felt sorry for her sons, but nobody was going to get away with saying I was an abusive mother. I could put up with her strange, weird habits and her outrageous garden; it never bothered me she was on the game, but to accuse me of hurting my kids was going too far.

The misogynist looked like Lurch from the Adams family, and he lived with his wife and three children. I know he knocked her about and would speak to her like shit. She walked behind him with her head down. We would hear him shouting at her, but I could not be bothered to get involved. Let her sort herself out like I had to leave the bastard. Reflecting on this, I feel ashamed, but she wasn't ready to move on, and I know she is still with him today.

The idiot was obsessed with me; he would spy through the fence if I was sunbathing, and if the kids were playing, he would say, "Shut up."

Of course, I told him to "Shut the fuck up, you prick".

Then he would try and be nice, saying, "If I can help you with anything".

The reply back was, "Fuck off."

Unbeknown to me, until many years later, the creep had placed a newspaper advert on my friend's car saying, 'Do you know she's an escort?' about me. I had lived there for ten years, and he was attempting to slander my name. I am 5'9/5'10 with long legs, whereas the bird on the advert was about 5'2; we shared the same haircut. I had managed to get a loan for home improvements, and builders were working on my house. He told people, including the builders, that under the floorboards, I had sex toys and a dungeon, and my name was Emma. Oh, c'mon -I'd think of something a bit sexier than that!

He complained to Environmental Health about the noise. Then he called the RSPCA about my dogs, saying I mistreated them and the council for anti-social behaviour. He would mutter names under his breath; you couldn't understand what he was saying, but then he turned and smiled as he rode by on his bike. Then, he wanted me to go with him as he was working on security for a well-known television drama. Are you mad, man? Every time he complained, I got the better of him, proving he was the one harassing me. He couldn't get one over on me, so I used to laugh at him in the end. Then, he would shout at his wife and kids.

With regards to the sex worker, I told her, "If any of your punters look at or approach my children, then you will see the ugly side of me."

One day, I got my own back; I was trimming my bushes in the garden, wearing a vest and cut-downs. I must have been on annual leave when I saw a young man get out of a lovely merc. 'Surely not - he's not going to fuck that!' I found myself thinking. Well, he looked at me, so I stuck my arse out, and when she opened the door, he shook his head and literally ran off. It was payback for me; I creased myself up and asked her if she was having a good day!

As I said before, the victim of domestic abuse is often a perpetrator. With the two neighbours, if they gave me grief, I learned to hit back hard. So when I bought a Landrover, I showed it off. They didn't know I had five years to pay for it. My kids always looked immaculate, and I walked out the door with my nose in the air. I just thought, 'Who the fuck are you to have a go at me and my family?'

I loved my house, but it's hard when things go wrong, and you're a single woman. I was new to the area, had no fresh contacts and made some bad mistakes. I hired a contractor to change every room: electrics, heating, flooring, and decorating after taking a twenty-five thousand pound re-mortgage.

When I hired him, I told him, "Don't take it for granted just because I'm on my own that I am a fool".

Within a couple of months, there was still no electricity or heating; I got him by the throat and threw his tools out of my house. He was later on the show "Cowboy Builders", so the little worm didn't get away with it.

We managed. Financially, it was hard, but I had three jobs, and I studied for six years doing various qualifications so we could have a better life. My Mum and Dad paid for trips and vocational courses as the children got older. We worked out that both Jimmy and Gus should have paid around thirty thousand pounds in maintenance each. They did not pay because I worked and refused to beg for money.

I was determined that my children would go away even for a weekend. I hated the caravan holidays, but the kids used to like seeing the characters dressed up in animal costumes. Georgina always took a friend, and they used to go off to the amusements. We would meet at various times in the park to eat or swim together. Usually, the weather was awful. At a caravan site in Kent, we were rocking with a mini tornado swirling around the coast. There was no electricity and no heating. We watched the caravans move and spray litter over the camp. Jake and Roma were two and four, so they were a little scared, but we played a game through it. This was one of my unforgettable adventures.

Jake was three when we first went abroad to Spain. It was hard as a single mum to carry luggage and tired children through airports. Jake was a mummy's boy; we even shared the same sunbed, so tanning wasn't my priority. Georgina was at the age where boys were important, so she and her friend would wiggle their little bums and boobs around the pool to get attention. Roma was a little daredevil, had a new best friend every day, and used to go to all the kids' clubs, greeting me with a little present or piece of artwork she had made. Jake was a little shy, so he sometimes stayed with me.

The holiday was relaxing until Roma hit her face on the side of the pool and required stitches. Poor baby, she still has a mark on her tooth due to the trauma of the accident. It happened at the end of the holiday, so she couldn't go into the pool anymore.

We had three holidays one year: one abroad and two weekends in a caravan and a chalet. Georgina was invited by a friend to go to America for three weeks, so with the help of my parents, we saved enough for her to go. That was the first time she was ever away from me, and I missed her so much and couldn't wait for her to come home. When we went overseas, we travelled mainly to European destinations. It was lovely when people asked them about travelling; they could provide a stamped passport with lovely memories to share.

The younger two also went to destinations with the school. As a younger child, Georgina always went with me and never wanted to sleep over at friends' houses. Twice, I had to pick her up late in the evening when she went to Brownie camps and then cried her little heart out to come home. We got the call, so Mum and I traipsed through cow shit and tripped over the molehills and rabbit burrows, walking in the middle of nowhere to get our baby back. All we had was a torch and plenty of mentions of 'never again', but we were laughing at the same time.

Roma and Jake were taken abroad courtesy of their grandmother's bank account. It worried me whether Gus should drink too much or if I panicked if they were kidnapped. But it was important for them to have a relationship with their father and sister. I also warned him I would take the next flight over if needed if they were upset. All my children were bought mobile phones from a very young age. Then, they could contact me at any time of the day or night. These children were my crown jewels; even today, they accuse me of being overprotective.

Roma, especially, used to miss me. As Jake became a little older, his delightful honesty would question that going with his Dad was embarrassing as he would steal the rolls from the breakfast bar and make them eat the rolls for lunch. My kids were not used to that! He used to accommodate them in a two-star hotel abroad or the cheapest caravan. Don't get me wrong, my kids are not spoiled, but there is no point in going away when you do not spend time and money on activities such as lunch out. Jake talks about his Dad's frugal habits, except when it comes down to him. He would walk about in designer clothes and steal breakfast rolls to feed his kids. They would run to me when I used to meet them at the airport.

Holidays and having childhood memories were important as my childhood lacked the yearly holiday. I had lovely memories of picnics on the field outside our house after school. I made sure our house was never empty, with a large swimming pool and bouncy castle - full of twenty screaming kids laughing and teenagers listening to music. I was happy if my children were happy! As a single parent, it was awkward when everyone else was with a partner. The father's absence was probably missed, but that was out of my control. My only control was to give them the best childhood possible. They deserved that.

20 | Internet Dating

Internet dating did not work well for me; the only reason I started this crazy way of meeting people was that others asked me to use my profile as they were finding it increasingly difficult to meet men. However, it was never hard for me to be asked out. I remember walking with my mum around Tesco with Jake and Roma. Suddenly, I felt that I was being followed by a tall man. Every time I took something from a shelf, I felt a long arm reach across. It wasn't until we were down the feminine hygiene aisle that I noticed he took some incontinence pads, now known as Tenor Lady. I looked up, and he dropped a packet, which led to packets sprawling over the floor. I began to laugh, and believe me when I laugh, it's filthy.

He came over to my trolley and said, "You do realise I have been trying to get your attention for the past twenty minutes, but I did not expect this to happen."

He said his name was Pete and asked mine. I looked in his trolley to see if there were any large family items, and he explained that he knew what I was looking for. He continued to say he was single, and by the way, was I? I had a three-year-old and an eighteen-month-old child in baby seats, shopping quietly with my mum.

I shouted to my mum, "He's trying to chat me up. What a bloody cheek."

She laughed and said, "Go for it; it's about time someone made you laugh".

Internet dating is very dangerous when you are vulnerable and lonely. There are many people out to scam you for a lot of money. They include gangs working outside the UK, taking on identities of people. One guy I was talking to, Edward White, was from a dating agency. This was a few years ago, so I hope they now verify true identities. I lent him three hundred pounds, but he wanted two thousand pounds to leave a foreign country. It was the old story - they pick a country you know from the media has plenty of corruption. They will tell you facts about the country that are true. Sometimes, you can tell you are not communicating with the same person by the slight differences in grammar and expression, but this is very discreet. He said he had travelled, so when I asked him how he had lost his original accent, this was his reasoning, and to be fair, people's accents do change. He sent me many photos of himself, a tall white man with a beard and reasonably good-looking. He then started contacting me crying, saying that he was in prison and needed more money. I found out where he was supposed to be and knew I needed to pursue this. I got a contact to meet him through a friend of a friend. When he turned the offer down, I called him a fake and told him to go and find another sucker.

They often use pay-as-you-go phones so they cannot be tracked. They sense vulnerability and ask questions so discreetly that you will answer them as they appear innocent. This is still going on, so just be very aware of what you are told through a screen and always have a backup plan when you meet someone. When you leave a violent and abusive relationship, you tend to become a rescuer and want to help other people who are in trouble. Be wise and not be fooled by these scammers.

After a while, my friend asked me to join a dating agency under a false name to support her. She was Asian, so there was no way she could get away with talking to the opposite sex. She just wanted a bit of banter. I went along with it, so I became Henrietta, the nurse. I was on a site for a day, and I just could not be bothered answering the messages, and my friend could not believe the chat-up lines and the amount of profile dick pics.

There was one guy who remained anonymous, obviously married! Many guys have no profile pics and are described as having no strings attached, wanting to have fun, etc. A guy called Neville, whose name says it all, began with non-flirty, intelligent messages. I asked why he did not expose his identity, and he explained that he was a lawyer just out of a marriage and was just intrigued by the idea of internet dating. I regularly started chatting to Neville for a couple of months, day-to-day shit. Still, he was intelligent, very amusing and different. We exchanged telephone numbers and finally agreed to meet up. Remember, I had no idea what this man looked like!

Georgina could now drive, and she was aware I was meeting up with him. We had a code, so she would rescue me at any point. I chose a local country pub, ten minutes away and only around the corner. Honestly, it was more of a friendship than the start of a romance for me. During the previous couple of months, I'd had an operation, and he had been so attentive and concerned throughout my recovery.

That night, I dressed casually in jeans, boots and a bodysuit, hair down, and wore a little bit of makeup. I entered the pub not knowing who I was meeting. It was fine, as I had an exit strategy. This man had never mentioned anything inappropriate sexually. All he said was that his ex was cold, and they never often had sex.

I looked around the pub; I thought I had been blown out when I heard a voice: "Henry, turn around".

I had to remember my fictitious name and turned around to see a small, skinny old man sitting on the couch. He looked like the fucking professor out of Bagpuss. Funny, isn't it? I did not have any recollection of age or class. He wore brown cords, a worn collar shirt and a cashmere jumper. His face was aged, and he had a long nose and horn-rimmed glasses. I was pissing myself inside but did not want to be rude, so I thought I'd have a couple of drinks, then call Georgina to get her arse down here.

Neville bought me a drink, I was not drinking alcohol, and we began to talk. He said I looked even more beautiful in the flesh, and he loved my long legs.

"Okay, thank you", I said, but I could not return the compliment.

I started talking about work and asked him whether he had ever represented anyone famous. This guy smelt of old money. Out of the blue, he said he had something to ask me.

"Go ahead", I said.

He said, "I would pay you a huge monthly sum of money."

Huh, I was intrigued but had no idea what was coming next.

"Can you wear stockings and suspenders and walk me around like a dog while I wear underpants?"

I was curious to know whether I heard him correctly. I paused, and then he carried on.

"Would it be possible for you to wear a strap-on penis and penetrate my anus"?

Yep, just like that, not even would you fuck my arse with a strap-on? I asked to be excused for a minute, made my way to the toilet and rang Georgina; fortunately, within minutes, I was picked up, and he was left in the pub. I also blocked his number from my phone. I did not know whether to laugh or be insulted. That skinny, ugly little rich man had the cheek to politely request I perform those kinky acts with him with a straight, earnest expression on his face.

Unfortunately, I did attempt internet dating again. This time, I was recovering from a bad migraine, lying in bed, feeling sorry for myself. I knew that life was changing for me and would be a bad time. I was vulnerable and lonely. I also was concerned that my injuries had now impacted my worst-case scenario of ending up in a wheelchair. I was due to have a hip replacement.

My worst fear was met with Colin; he was a tall, muscular firefighter. He had been in the Air Force and had experienced a bad childhood. Why did I not read the signs? He took me out and treated me like a lady, so we dated for about eighteen months. I was on heavy medication, so I was happy for him to look after me. He was so helpful, especially with my finances (note sarcasm); we went on holiday, and I paid. Whenever we went out, I paid, and then he wanted to live with me. During this time, after my major operation and taking morphine, he asked me to lend him money, and I did. We even set up a joint bank account just before my operation. I could not have sex due to my disability, and what man would put up with that? I was continuously on high pain relief, and at times, I had an epiphany and asked why he never put his hands in his wallet. He would then get defensive. Oh yes, by the way, he was also a compulsive liar. What a catch! He said he was being paid to do some dodgy work to earn extra money. I asked no questions, but I remember once he came back with a huge cut on his head.

Being a firefighter, he would often be on shifts, but he showed me where he lived, with a friend in a house in Oxfordshire. So, I was sure he was not in a relationship. Still, my mind was so full elsewhere that I did not see his lying, deceitful behaviours until I had my operation due to the medication and pain I was in. Within two months, I was very much clued up and told him to fuck off after lying to Roma about something trivial. And another thing, his breath stunk like shit, so I also told him that. I was never repaid the money. There was a time when I was desperate and needed it, so I asked him, and he said he had been diagnosed with lung cancer due to passive inhalation of chemicals from his job. That was really weird because I know for a fact, after a little digging around, that he's still in the fire service and working. Something about him was uneasy and dangerous, so I felt it was best to let the money go and leave him to his lies and stinking rotten breath.

I did give the internet another few tries; after all, like I said, the loneliness creeps up on you. So, I met this guy on a date. He was funny, and I dated him for a few weeks.

We went out for meals and drinks, and after a while, the end-of-the-night kiss could have turned into a little more until he said, "Hey, you know what really turns me on about you?"

I asked, expecting a cheeky comment.

"Your arse! I would really like you to shit in my mouth".

This fucking geezer was a professional in a high-ranking job, and he wanted me to shit in his mouth. What the fuck was going on in this world with these men? They are seriously fucked up! He had the cheek to call three years later via a different number. WHY?

I have been out on a few dates via the internet. Some men were extremely polite, and I enjoyed talking to them. But on the dates, it always turned to sexual innuendos. They try to touch you or expect something at the end of the date. They usually tell you a story about a woman who has either cheated on them, was crazy, or stole their money. All I ever asked for was respect and to be treated with kindness.

Some men wanted a full-on relationship, which I never had time for; my family always came first. Others appear really full-on and then start making excuses as to why they don't ring for a while. Another red flag, so they go. I have only loved two men in my life, and they ended up treating me like shit. So now, I tend to have less patience in pursuing or trying to rescue; it's all about loving myself more now.

21 | Drugged

I'd had to have a minor hip operation to put on hold any more extensive surgeries. The doctor and I were unsure they would work, but it had been worth taking the risk. It was six months later, and I felt good and confident. Georgina said it was about time that we went out for a drink. It had been a while since I wore a dress and heels and felt good about myself. My consultant told me that the previous operation should last about five years. I had a few scars on the top of my thigh, but generally, I felt amazing.

Georgina always styled my hair for nights out, and Roma, who was always good with make-up, ensured I felt confident in a skimpy backless dress. I was not driving that night, so Georgina encouraged me to have alcohol. I knew I would be in the right company to drink; we would have a few drinks and go home. My friend Oliver, whose job was to protect the public, said he would be coming off shift when the club finished, so he would pick us up.

I had known Oliver for almost four years, and he often popped over to discuss his relationship with his current girlfriend. I was not seeing anybody, so I often gave him advice and was a shoulder to cry on as his mother had a terminal illness. He had shagged many of the females at his work. I knew Oliver fancied me but respected my wishes; on many occasions, I did not know about his indiscretions. Oliver had once asked me to go out for a ride with him and tried to kiss me; he also stated that he was in love with me. I just laughed at him and said he was a little emotional over his mum and that I wasn't the right person for him. I was flattered but really did not take any notice. I also felt safe with Oliver; he had my back, and I trusted him.

We had a good night, fuelled with alcohol, and I enjoyed dancing for the first time in a couple of years. It was a beautiful evening in June, so it was nice to come out of the club and not wait for a cab. I was a little intoxicated, but not that bad. I was aware of everything going on inside and outside the club. A few girls were arguing, but Georgina and I just laughed and saw our lift home. It didn't take long for us to get to Georgina's house, and the last thing she said to him was, "Look after my mum and make sure she gets home safe."

He assured her he would, and we went to my house.

I don't know how it happened, but he asked if he could come in and use the toilet. I felt a little cloudy and remember dropping my keys on the kitchen floor. He picked them up and said I needed some water, and he went to the tap and poured some for me to drink.

The next thing I recall was lying on my stomach, and I felt my legs being pulled back off the bed like a nutcracker. The pain was unbearable, and I screamed, then felt no more. Then I was lying on him, and his head was underneath me. I could faintly hear him moaning underneath the lower part of my body. But it felt like a dream; I was in and out of consciousness. I then came round and saw his face; he kissed the top of my head, and he was gone. I then went back to my unconscious state.

I woke up late afternoon to my phone ringing, but I never answered; Georgina, who was checking up on me to see if I was okay, left a message. I returned the call. I felt like I had been hit over the head; my brain felt completely fried, but I was naked. I quickly got off the phone with Georgina, and I didn't mention anything as my head was very fuzzy. Roma and Jake had slept at a friend's house, so they would not return till later. All I felt was pain in my hip. I kept getting weird flashbacks of the corkscrew position and him underneath me. I always showered or bathed before bed, but I could see heavy makeup residue on my skin, and my hair was matted. To this day, I can't remember anything else. I have tried to rewind to coming home and drinking a glass of water, what happened after that, and how I got into my bed. I don't remember taking off my dress. All I knew was that I was in such terrible pain and felt sick to my stomach.

I sat down on the stairs, and suddenly, the realisation of what had happened made me sob hysterically. I had been drugged, but when? Had it happened in the car, or was it in the glass of water? The worst thing is, to this day, I still don't know what that bastard did to me.

A couple of hours later, I received a message from him. He said, 'We had a good time, and anytime you want a lift, let me know,' followed by a heart emoji. I had been raped by Jimmy many times, and I remember it all and how he used violence. I had been raped by Gus, and I remember every time it had happened aside from Jake's conception. I did not know what Oliver saw or what he did to me; I did not have any marks on my body. I don't know if he penetrated me. This was far worse because I could not remember.

I telephoned Georgina, apologised for ending the earlier phone call and told her what had happened.

She first said, "But mum, you weren't drunk; we were both fine in the car."

I explained I did not feel sore anywhere apart from my hips. As someone who was dancing the night before, I felt it was difficult to walk. He then texted me later on, and I was so angry. I replied back, 'You know what you did, you fucking cunt.' I then blocked him; he wasn't going to admit to it. I had two choices: go to the police or try and forget about it.

As his work was to protect the public in an authoritative role, I knew I would be made to look like a bad person. The drunken slut that has turned - I had heard it in the various conversations relating to rape. He had been to my house, and I had been in his car before the incident. My history would be pulled out with the various court cases. I had been raped many times, so why would I want to go through that again. He would get his hand slapped behind closed doors and possibly a transfer. I would be the face that cried rape. I only needed to go to the doctor to get checked out the next day. Afterwards, I kept bathing and washing myself. I stuck soap inside my vagina and tried to get any traces of him out. I scrubbed my anus just in case he stuck it up there.

I felt sick and shocked and sat rocking and trying to get the humiliation and pain out of my body. But I felt dirty and angry. I wanted to fucking go and kill the bastard; he was supposedly my friend. How could he do this to me? Had I led him on? I went through this with Georgina, and she confirmed "that dirty bastard drugged you, Mum, and raped you" and "it wasn't your fault. He's a rapist, and something needs to be done about it."

I was tired of my body being used as a sexual vessel; I could not remember anything other than a few flashbacks. I was so sick of men abusing me; I just wanted to be left alone.

The following day, I went to work limping; my colleague noticed that I was pale and sensed something was wrong.

"Why are you limping? Are you okay?"

We went somewhere private, and I told him what had happened.

"Darling, you need to go to the police; how many other people has he done this to?"

I broke down and said I couldn't do this anymore. I could not go to the police but needed to see a doctor. My line manager was a male, and I felt embarrassed and humiliated trying to explain what had happened. 'Should I have known better? I am a woman in her forties and have a granddaughter. How could I let this happen to me again?' The team manager was a woman, so I told her what had happened. She advised that I was in no fit state to work; I needed to be examined and go to the police.

She put her arm around me and said, "You need to go home; you can't work like this; go see the GP and then decide how you will play this".

That afternoon, I went to see my own GP; Georgina came with me. I started to cry when I told him what had happened and said I felt so stupid and humiliated. I said that

I needed some strong painkillers to ease my hip joint. He kindly advised me to go to the police. I raised my voice.

"He has authority in his job; they won't believe me; think of my dignity."

He then asked me to lie on the bed as he needed to examine me. He lifted my skirt to my knees, and I became hysterical that another man was going to touch me again. I begged him to leave me alone; of course, he could see how distressed I was. He referred me to the clinic where I would be given tests to see if I had contracted an STI and if there were any traces of Rohypnol. However, it was unlikely there would be signs of any drug as it was over seventy-two hours since it occurred. He felt confident that I had been drugged due to my lack of memory and the fact I had not consumed much alcohol.

Georgina supported me to the dirty clinic, as I called it. I had an examination by the nurse, and they confirmed after three days that I had no sexual infection. The only thing that was left was my disappointment for men.

I saw Oliver about six weeks later, in Tesco's. He called my name, and as I turned, I saw the face of someone who was once my friend, who had since raped me. Normally, I would fight my way out of any situation. As I looked into his big brown eyes, I began to shake; my legs could not move, and I stared at him, speechless. It felt like minutes, but it was only probably seconds before he turned away. I could not move until I saw him at the end of the aisle; I put my shopping down on the floor and limped out. That monster had also caused an injury to the operated side of my hip. All the hard work of the surgeon, the healing and my confidence was now fucked due to this fucking monster. Why? Because the only way he could touch me was by raping me after having drugged me. What enjoyment could anyone get out of someone incapacitated and not in control? I answered my own question - he was in control.

22 | Finances

I lost my home in 2014 as I could not maintain the mortgage anymore and have been privately renting ever since. My gold had been pawned over the years, so I had nothing to sell; my health had deteriorated, so I could not earn extra money, and I was not entitled to any help as a homeowner. I could not change my mortgage or meet my priority debts. I was a manager then but had to reluctantly get a food parcel to survive and was at risk of losing my home. The irony was I was working with people on benefits who had far more than me.

I did not want to go to the district council and pronounce I was fleeing domestic abuse from Gus at the time. I had to go into accommodation after Jimmy, which I would never have chosen but at the time for which I was deeply grateful. This time, I wanted to keep my independence and dignity. The night before I was due to leave our family home, I kept thinking about the first night, sitting on the sofa, thinking it was mine. I had achieved this. The only thing I had achieved was selling it to a greedy landlord at fifty thousand pounds below the asking price so I could pay my debts and have some leftover money.

We went to live in a smaller three-bedroom house. I took the smallest room to give them enough space, and it had only been recently decorated, but it did not feel like home to us. I wanted to provide them with a desired home or a good-sized deposit. Instead, I bought two cars, one for Georgina and me, as she needed one. I paid off my mum and debts, which left me with about ten thousand pounds to spare. I should have invested it, but I never. Roma and Jake had a fabulous year, often leading to us shopping a lot. They had new beds and TVs, playstations, bikes, and anything they wanted but the security of me owning a house. I felt guilty for them, but they never moaned about leaving Bexley Road.

At the time, Georgina was in a relationship with Joe, pregnant with Mabel, and had her own place. When Mabel was born, Georgina had severe post-natal depression, and this meant that I had to be hands-on with her. Georgina felt she could not bond with her and went through a terrible time. Joe was an arsehole, immature and did not support her throughout this whole experience. It was difficult, and he often would leave her when she was at her most vulnerable. My attention was on my daughter and my grandchild at the time; she needed that stability as she was healing from a very difficult birth, and she was exhausted and frustrated as she didn't feel happy about being a Mum. It felt strained and did not come naturally at the start.

She overcame this and built a wonderful relationship with her now three children, Mable, Martha and Callum. She has herself experienced many obstacles but has achieved so much.

Georgina and her partner Joe have had several uncomfortable years but have chosen to stick through it and plan to get married.

23 | My Soulmate

I met Simon at the start of August 2019; he had arranged to inspect my rental property. From the moment I looked at his face, it re-ignited a spark within seconds like he was someone I felt I had known for years. Immediately, we started talking about his plans to move abroad within the next few years. At that time, I had been seeing someone for a few weeks, so there wasn't any commitment, and Simon said he was single. He was from Southern Ireland and had the most beautiful voice ever. He was different to anyone I had met, and I fell for his charm; within a week, I had finished with the guy I was seeing and he asked me out.

Our first date was a meal at the local pub; he insisted on drinking tap water, which seemed a little weird, and he barely ate. I put it down to his nerves. This man was amazing; I instantly felt comfortable and attracted to him. It was like we'd met in a previous life and were restarting in another. He met my family, and we spent a wonderful Christmas together; he bought me a Claddagh ring and promised to love me forever. I was smitten and in love for the first time since Jimmy, but this was a grown-up love, something so beautiful and amazing that you often read about but never believe it would happen to you.

We had a couple of mishaps - an ex tried to call him a couple of times, and he agreed to meet up with her. He had experienced eighteen years of an unhappy marriage, which was on and off for many years. He had two children, and sometimes their relationship appeared strained, but he said it was his ex who had brainwashed them over the years, so at times, he would come across as guarded. I believe everyone holds something from past experiences, so I took this with a pinch of salt.

We spent time together after Christmas, too, and then he sent me a text ending the relationship. I was in pieces and asked for an explanation. He said it was not working, saying he had spoken to his family, and they all decided for him to end it. I was shocked and in despair. There was no real explanation after our last few incredible months together. Our love life and everything was perfect. What happened to us? Where had it all gone wrong? The love of my life had disappeared. I felt he was my soulmate, and I loved him from the bottom of my heart. Once again, I felt so alone. It felt different this time; there was no abuse and no real explanation. There wasn't any closure, and I felt so confused.

Two months later, I had a fault at the house, and my landlord advised me to contact Simon. I had no choice, so I reluctantly had to contact him again. Immediately, when we were back in the room, it felt electric again; he said it had been a mistake and he had missed me. I was the love of his life. For the past few months, COVID enforced that we were sometimes restricted from seeing each other, but we picked up where we left off after the first lockdown. He said he had wobbled and was scared, so he ended the relationship. I was in love with this man; he was my soul mate, so I believed him. He was the one for me.

Simon was happy to do anything for me; I thought our love was mutual; everything was perfect; he was attentive, loyal, generous, handsome, sexy - just so perfect. Our sex life was off the scale. He insisted on making sure I was satisfied with his love-making skills, totally selfless. But as always, there are red flags in any relationship, and I was so blinded by love that I totally refused to see them.

When we split up, Simon bought shares in a business but lacked business skills. So, as a commitment to our future, and with the expectation we would save to buy a house together, we agreed I would work without a wage. I became the single point of contact, answered the phone, and passed on the accounts, invoices, etc. I was more than happy to work together, and after a full day's work and on weekends, I would work for the business. It was thriving, and Simon often slipped a few quid in my purse. Although I worked seven days a week, I was happy with the decision. He was so good to me.

I saw Simon roughly three times a week for two years, and they were wonderful; we were so much in love, and everyone was happy with this man who brought the smile back on my face again after so many years. My grandchildren adored him, and he spent time taking them out. I was so proud to be with this beautiful, handsome, adorable man and wanted to spend the rest of my life with him. We were a partnership, blissfully happy and planning for the rest of our lives together.

One day whilst reviewing a text message from a customer, I saw a message from Simon and online photos showing dick pics. In her text, the customer was not interested, but Simon pursued her. Upon seeing this, I challenged Simon, who proclaimed his innocence and said he was lonely when we broke up. The context of the message was like a dagger going through my heart. He was calling her beautiful; the compliments were out of this world. He'd said the same to me. After this incident, I never believed him when he complimented me, and I should have finished it there and then. But as he reminded me, we'd been on a break, so I fell for his line of loneliness and swept it away but did not forget. This is exactly how we met, so I was always on high alert after this.

Simon was also a weed smoker, but although I had my suspicions, he assured me he rarely drank. His children told me stories of him passing out through drink and drugs, but once again, I was so in love with this man and did not see this side of him. I put it down to bitterness and maybe a little resentment and jealousy. He promised me he would never cheat and admitted to looking at porn. Between the lockdowns, he was visited by a friend and his new girlfriend. The next day, he accused me of flirting with him, an accusation which came out of the blue. He then apologised and blamed his ex-wife as she was constantly having affairs, so I felt this was perfectly acceptable under the circumstances. I always felt awkward in his friend's company, so I avoided him, and then when he stayed over again, this time with his ex-partner, I made an excuse not to meet with them.

The alcohol was a difficult one to measure. If Simon drank, and this was a rare occasion, he became pissed very quickly, and I could not understand why. He would say it was because he never ate. I have lived with drinkers, totally aware of all the signs, but once again refused to accept my perfect man had a problem.

I worked extremely hard trying to fit in life with my family, my relationship with Simon at weekends, working for the business daily, taking calls, and twice a week spending hours writing quotes and invoices and communicating with the accountants, banks, etc. I noticed that Simon was not attending the appointments with customers and was making excuses, saying he had an emergency to sort out. Calls were often received as the jobs were not getting fixed properly, and he had to go back sometimes multiple times to complete the tasks and make good. I challenged Simon about this; he had lost a few contracts, and the business had begun to suffer. I then noticed Simon was only working two to three days a week. I wondered what he was doing as I was working around the clock. This led to conflict, but I could never get to the bottom of it.

He also bought a van to convert into a camper van, but it remained outside for over a year and was never completed. We'd planned to travel and, at times, with the grandchildren and have mini breaks and holidays. My reassurance was COVID-19; I always made an excuse for him.

In 2021, I noticed I became awfully tired and my stomach bloated. Covid impacted the health agencies, so my Dad agreed to pay for a private consultant, who advised I had been prescribed the wrong medication for three years. This had impacted our sex life, as I did not feel sexy anymore. Being the gentlemen, Simon booked a short break to

Cornwall for us to get away. I was also suffering with my left hip, making exercise really difficult for me, but just spending time away with Simon was what I needed. Nothing was too much trouble for him. He would massage my limbs, give me pedicures, and never moan if I went to bed early. He started complaining a little about us not kissing or the lack of affection. But kissing led to sex, and my movements were so limited.

Simon then started commenting about my male Facebook friends. He had female friends and was always working in people's houses; some were exes. Our relationship was never toxic; we had an honest relationship where it was acceptable to ask awkward questions and sometimes discuss issues outside of both of our comfort zones. One thing I did notice, but never questioned Simon about, was when we had sex, he would be in the middle of performing and then quickly revert his attention to foreplay. I never complained as he was never a selfish lover, and I would never have embarrassed him, so I kept quiet.

The drive to Cornwall was pleasurable - we passed Stonehenge and stopped at a greasy spoon to eat. The B&B was basic but clean, and due to COVID restrictions, restaurants were often booked up for weeks in advance, so it was hit-and-miss. Simon loved walking and admiring the beautiful landscape. It hurt me to walk, and I found it boring, sitting in multiple fields watching him smoking weed and zoning out. I like the hustle and bustle of town and people-watching. We found somewhere to eat, and he made reservations at a Michelin-star restaurant for another night. That evening, we stopped off to look at the stars on the way back to the B&B, but it became cold, so I returned to sit in the car. The same night, I reacted badly to the food and felt unwell the next day. Simon was fully aware that I was in discomfort and appeared as attentive as ever.

One morning, after having his morning smoke, Simon received a call notifying him that he had lost a big contract; this obviously impacted his mood; he snapped when I was not ready to go out and accused me of talking to one of my male friends on the phone. He also commented that this holiday was supposed to be about us being intimate, and I felt pressured for the first time. After driving and visiting more countryside, I asked him if we could go home a day early. I was fed up with fields and wanted to see my family.

On the way home, the conversation was strained; it did not occur to me that we needed to reflect and discuss our differences. Many couples have different hobbies and lifestyles, so it did not take away our love. We had so much to look forward to, and we could overcome anything by communicating. The following month was Georgina's wedding. This occasion was beautiful; he looked handsome and was amazing with my grandchildren. In the pre-wedding run-up, attending a fitting with Georgina, Simon had even bought me a wedding dress; we were planning to get married, and he never officially proposed but saw a dress, asked me to try it on and bought it for me. But like everything with Simon, he never saw anything through properly. He always was very impulsive, but I liked that about him.

Christmas came and went. Meeting up with loved ones was difficult, and Simon wanted to go to Southern Ireland to see his family. Whilst cooking one day, I suffered serious burns to my back and lower part of my body. Simon drove me to the hospital for weekly check-ups and changed my dressings. He found our dwindling sex life frustrating as I couldn't be touched. Due to the trauma of being burnt and the size of my kitchen, we decided to move in together, making it easier to save for a deposit to buy our own home. Simon worked incredibly hard to get a deposit together. I managed the office so we could rent a larger house to move two families into one house. Simon said the spare room would be available for his kids as he did not want them moving in with us. He was happy for them to live with their mum.

Simon planned to buy me an engagement ring; he wanted me to be involved, and we went out to design the perfect ring. He informed his family, who sent us gifts to celebrate this event. There was one problem: he could not afford the ring and needed to save for it. This was fine; I would have worn tin foil if it meant I could marry this man.

We found a house and began to plan to move from two houses into one. It was exciting, and we were both looking forward to the next stage in our life. The weekend we were supposed to move, my boxes were all packed. All we needed to do was clean once everything had been moved out. Simon needed to take down the shed in my house, where he had previously stored some of his tools. There would be an overlap of moving between the two houses of a day for Simon and three weeks for my house.

Covid restrictions had finally lifted, and Simon's friends had decided to drift back into his life again. I wasn't keen on some; they were immature and acted like fools, encouraging Simon to go on drinking and smoking binges. Some of the friends were single, womanisers and smokers. One group of friends called themselves 'the three amigos'. I have another name for them, and it's not pleasant.

Simon was a grown man, and he was accountable for his choices. One of these friends invited himself to stay with Simon the weekend before moving. I wasn't very happy about it, knowing it was the weekend to pack up. That weekend, he left his flat in a total mess; the day of moving, these friends, who I assumed were helping, never showed up. It was down to us to move. Fortunately, we had help from my family. Simon expected everyone to chip in and moaned at my daughter, who went for a walk. This surprised me.

Before I arrived at the new house, he ensured that a bottle of champagne and a sash to cut were ready to celebrate our new start. It was stressful and overwhelming, like any house move, and I was suffering from pain in my hip and excruciating burns that covered my body. I probably wasn't as responsive as I should have been.

The next day, we prepared to move out of his flat. It was dirty and totally disorganised, and it was clear he had spent the weekend boozing. I directed the cleaning and organised the flat for several hours, obviously annoyed at him. Then, at the end of the day, he informed me that he needed to return the truck in forty-five minutes or lose his deposit. We managed to do it, but the consequences of this caused more damage to my hip and pain down my legs. From this moment, things began to turn downhill. He began to question my fidelity daily when I only had love for this man. He accused me of uploading sexualised pictures on Facebook. It became so bizarre that, at first, I laughed, but I became increasingly annoyed and frustrated. He also accused me of flirting with other men I worked with professionally. I became nervous at mentioning a male name; he listened to work conversations and made ludicrous comments.

Within a month of moving in, I found out a lot. Simon had been messaging another woman he had met through work, allegedly providing help with our relationship. He had an open business Instagram page with porn displayed on it and was following other women. I did not handle this very well. I caught him drunk after drinking a bottle of vodka in the shed, so I attacked him verbally and defended myself. This was the man who I loved with all my heart; I was beyond despair. He also continued to talk to the woman, proclaiming his innocence. He felt that my children should pay more rent and be more responsible for cleaning the house. Simon cleaned the house once; Simon never paid for food and yet secretly ate after everyone went to bed. This man I adored was drinking alcohol and smoking weed openly in the garden. I found empty bottles of vodka, and anything he could drink, he would.

He started staying away for nights and weekends, coming home in the early hours. He ignored me; the man that had been so attentive looked through me. He also informed me that after years of being together, he used to take blue pills as he was having problems with erectile dysfunction. We spent time talking about it, and he said he had been on the pills for years. I was confused; we'd never had any problems in the bedroom, but suddenly, it all made sense to me. He would take the pills before I visited him; I did not know whether to feel sorry for him or annoyed due to the years I had been deceived. He became very sneaky and commented inappropriately, especially to Roma, but never in my presence. Ultimately, I had no choice but to say I was done! It had finished.

Simon moved into the spare room, stopped paying the rent and left one Sunday morning. He demanded money back from the deposit. Everything appeared to be a lie. How could this man change from an absolute god to someone I did not recognise? According to him, his friends encouraged him to move out, and to this day, I do not know but fear who he has become. I do not know where it went wrong, only that I ignored the warning signs. How can someone change so quickly?

He sent me a message threatening legal action if I refused to return the wedding dress, knives, coffee machine, and some towels. To avoid any trouble, I gave him back everything and advised him never to speak to me or my family again.

A couple of weeks later, he turned up on my door, stating I had some mail, which I never received. He explained that it had taken him a lot to come and see me. He then started shouting and swearing at the front door, so I slammed the door in his face. I called my friend for her to witness this man's voice and to talk to her. He had never been violent or abusive. Every couple of weeks, he contacted me asking for something else. Something trivial.

I then managed to block him from everything. I received a call from the police stating I had stolen his phone. I denied it; this was the phone I used to take his work calls, and it was over two years old. The police then said it was a civil matter and advised me to return his phone. I explained how he was harassing me! I felt humiliated, as though I had done something very wrong, but I handed the phone over. I advised them to inform him never to contact me again.

A few weeks later, I received a call stating he wanted the deposit back and to surrender the tenancy. So, to avoid any trouble, I signed a new tenancy and handed over a new deposit. And waited for the next instruction.

He never contacted me again, and I have now moved into a new house. The previous house was full of memories and meant nothing anymore to me. I had been taught a new lesson. This man encouraged me to start writing this book again after his parting reaction to me was, 'You're an author; you are good at exaggerating the truth.' If I had bollocks, then this was a kick in them! He knew about the nightmares I had experienced and the abuse I had suffered. To this day, there has not been any closure. I had fallen in love with a man who did not exist. I genuinely thought he was the one.

The pain in my heart hangs like it reaches the intense acid of the stomach. My brain is entwined with leaves of a vine which suffocates the beautiful leaves of the lily. Memories of lips moving slowly give pleasure to the symmetrical unknown to others. Hands that can damage but treat the skin as glass. Slowly, the pain and scars disappear in the night hours, closely guarded by a body of steel.

The mind appears so fragile; it listens to the thunder and not the trickle of dew. The outrage of Thor minimises the juices of Venus. The sun does not appear from the heavy storm clouds crashing and banging, making it impossible to release the warmth of the sun. There are signs of a rainbow, but the storm returns.

The ice on the lake, shall I step on it? Will it break and fall to the deepness of slime, or is it safe to cross? Can the pen allow her cygnets to cross, or does she look for her cob to define the task? Will the ice thaw in time, or does she remain on the bank, safe but alone?

A new life is born; do we appear as one? Does life end when there is no air to share? Love is a memory, a lesson of life, scars that depict despair invisible to the eye of the unworthy. Only the one can soothe.

The memories of love between the sheets
Will remain until one day we meet
The devastation of the drama
The reflection of such past karma.
Your persistence of money
But your ways are so funny
You destroyed faith with the lies
No choice but to remove the ties
Enemies, friends or foe
It's all about gossip, but with nowhere to go
The gaslighting continued, suicidal thoughts
The emotional abuse
Continuous alcohol and substance misuse
Being in love is our human nature
To help the lost soul is my empathetic nature
But my world once again is upside down
I'm still full of anger, and no smiles
Just a frown
You promised to protect me
Keep me safe, avoid all harm
But the crisis remained and sounded alarms
I am a survivor - strong, undefeated
There is a part of sheer incompleteness.
The hole in my heart is opened wide
Self-respect and dignity to restore my own pride
But another day is the same as before,
Full of silence from that voice I adore
No cross-cutting wit or silly smile
The mistakes of life are in constant denial.

I left that door open for you to walk back
But you found the words to hurt and attack
So, each day, I wait in total suspense
Was our relationship just full of pretence?

24 | Regrets and Casualties

I have two main regrets in my life: one is having the abortion, and two, giving up my home. With regards to the abortion, I have lost so many babies, so by having that removed, I will never forgive myself. Yet I do mourn about those pregnancies that did not make it. I carry around the guilt, knowing that the violence and emotional abuse may have taken its toll on my body and caused damage to my unborn children.

I went on to have two more children with Gus after Georgina had arrived from my time with Jimmy; no, they were not planned, and yes, I did take the morning-after pill with Roma. Jake, was my tenth and last pregnancy; anyone who has lost babies will understand how difficult it is to write about this. But I call them my wonderful surprises. I do not regret having my babies, and my proudest achievement is watching them grow as they mature into adults, acknowledging the sacrifices made for their happiness. Georgina said that I often looked sad and stressed when she was growing up, which I apologise for allowing her to see. As parents, we are human, and I have tried to protect them from my tears and anger over the years. My children are my most valued and prized successes.

There have been times when it has been difficult as a family. I regret allowing Roma and Jake to see their father, but I thought he would do a better job than Jimmy. Georgina said she felt left out sometimes at Christmas and birthdays as Jimmy did not bother with her. My mum has always spoilt Georgina; as a child, she had at least two birthday parties a year, countless phones and designer clothes, but it did not stop her pain from missing her dad. Gus knew that I would not stop him from seeing the children, as Jimmy not seeing Georgina regularly left a permanent scar. Gus knew how she felt when she would have to do a Grandad's Father's Day card instead of one for her Dad. During arguments, he would ask her, "Where's your dad?" I immediately stood by my daughter, but I had two other kids who wanted to see their father.

Both Roma and Jake chose not to see their father at the ages of fourteen and fifteen. I tried to protect them. As children, they were protected from the countless incidents and the vile times with him; after he raped me, I would come out of the room, smile at the two beautiful faces looking up at me excited for seeing their Dad. His behaviour has impacted Roma; he let her down throughout her life, but she feels guilty and confused as she never said goodbye to him after he was found lying dead on the floor in 2020. Neither of them saw him before he died, but out of respect, both went to the funeral. Both recall their last memories of him deceiving them about his intake of alcohol, turning up to football matches drunk, and calling them names when they stuck up for their mum. This resulted in their relationship diminishing. His last phone call to his son was to tell him to change his surname, as he didn't belong to him. I had to block his number as he tried to harass me with his inappropriate comments. Jake would often take the phone and tell him to fuck off and leave us alone and refers to him as Gus and not Dad.

We have videos of them with Gus in the early days on special occasions, and they reflect on his behaviour and see what a pig he was. He had previously been detained under the Mental Health Act and was suffering from sclerosis of the liver.

Jimmy was sometimes residing in Her Majesty's accommodation and had been homeless. He did not know his daughter and did not recognise her at a family party.

My own Dad died in 2022 and admitted later in life that he was an alcoholic, but he never regretted it - it was the norm to drink. I love and miss my Dad, and now I accept that he wasn't aware of what was going on; his needs came first due to his addiction. My Mum is our rock. She is our queen. Before Dad died, we talked a lot; there was a lot more to him, secrets he may have taken to the grave. But he is a huge void in my life as he also became my protector and advisor. I always told him I loved him despite his constant singing of songs relating to anything that was going on in my life. He was a very intelligent man, and addiction affected not only him but the rest of us, too.

Now, all three kids drive reasonable cars; I bought each a car, and my Dad paid for their driving lessons, so not having that father figure has impacted them practically. Emotionally, I am not so sure. When you are in an abusive relationship and have children, the perpetrator will often use the tactic of trying to make you feel that you are not a good enough mother. This emotional abuse is a pattern to shame you, so you depend on what little they offer. You are often blamed for everything that happens to the perpetrator, even after you have left them. Sometimes, you will not have the money to pay for the latest phone or designer trainers, but by showing them that with a good work ethic, things will eventually come. All my children are employed and undertaking additional college courses. Single parents often are used as an example for low attainment and poor attendance at school. They are at times stigmatized but I use this term very strongly and abuse does not discriminate throughout this book. If you manage to be strong enough to get out of an abusive relationship, please take time to think about yourself and your children.

Jimmy was a product of his own childhood, which is very sad. He was a beautiful but dangerous man; he never loved me but tried to control me. Gus was a spoilt little brat and was suffocated by a woman who had her own mental health problems. He often saw her being sectioned as a child but did not respect women or his own children. His addiction and needs came first.

Perpetrators come in all different shapes and sizes. They will do anything to humiliate you, remove every ounce of dignity that you once owned and then will go on to the next relationship and will abuse that one. They will sniff out the victim's vulnerability and use it to their advantage. This does not only happen to women, but it can also happen to men. It does not just happen to people in heterosexual relationships but also applies to same sex partnerships or any way a person wishes to identify themself as.

Research says the most dangerous time is when you leave the relationship, but I am unsure. The perpetrator will come back time after time using their vile techniques to display their control. Day-to-day abuse often occurs in an abusive relationship, the dreaded feeling of their feet coming up the stairs or the key turning in the lock. Will the dinner be eaten, or will the wall catch it tonight? How am I going to face people tomorrow and cover that bruise up? Who will be judging me? How can I get the kids ready and off to school without bumping into that nosey teacher who will ask questions? Are my kids going to be removed if I tell anyone?

When someone is constantly telling you how useless you are and putting you down, prodding, poking, punching, sometimes - retaliation is the only comfort. Sometimes, I would answer back or laugh at another blow or kick. I would be compared to other people's wives and girlfriends, so I would remind him how shit in bed he was! Or, one day, I would find someone better than him. Of course, this would be a red flag to a bull, so consequently, I was made to suffer for my comments for days or weeks. This was an excuse to call me a slag or a slut and say that I deserved to get raped or roughed up during sex. I deserved the embarrassing threat of an image being tied to every lamppost so the people around the school could see how much of a slut I was.

I was also often subjected to the light being turned on and off at night because if he wasn't sleepy, why should I sleep? Or making a loud bang, so you would jump out of your skin. It's not surprising Georgina was and still is such a light sleeper. I know I should have left, but I was scared, as he threatened to ruin my face or Georgina could be without her Mum and dead.

I was never allowed to be ill or mourn after losing my babies; every night was my turn to get up and feed. The endless amount of sickness, shitty nappies and the fact that Georgina wasn't a very good sleeper meant I was exhausted. I was ill most of the time, suffering from anaemia, but constantly being told how useless I had become, as it was natural for most women to have children and keep a home. So, for a while, I gave up and became a zombie, the words firing off my frail body, sick of the abuse and sleep deprivation, but doing the best I could.

It was not enough. And yes, I still went to work, slapped on my makeup, and smiled through my pain. Because my babies needed me, and despite the awful words, harassment via text messages, constant phone calls and put-downs, I carried on.

After a busy day at work and studying, my kids often chilled or fell asleep in bed. I would treat myself to some sanctuary - a bath, but it hasn't always been that pleasant. My only piece of solitude and comfort was in the bath, where I could shut my eyes and feel the bubbles cleansing my mind or mostly soothing the bruises. It also got rid of the sex smell that seemed to last for days at a time.

Often, memories distorted my harmonious time in the bath; I would suddenly be disturbed and told to get out. If I didn't get out quickly enough, a toilet brush would be thrown into the water. Other times, I would be urinated over. It was like I couldn't be left at peace; I was always accused of planning something or planning to meet someone.

And when you do escape, what exactly are you escaping? The impact of abuse is still there, manipulating how you appear or relate to others. How do you tell a colleague, or someone you don't really trust, that you were raped in the kitchen at the weekend? The door shut, and the kids were told to go and play while he talked to mummy; if you attacked back or caused a scene, it would upset the kids as he would refuse to have them, and they were so looking forward to seeing him? How many Christmases' and birthday parties have I been smiling while cutting the cake, feeling his dirty semen running down my legs, blissfully hoping nobody could see a damp patch. I wanted to hang my head in shame, and he would mouth, 'You're a slag' or 'Slag'. Who do you trust to get away? Because I guarantee, especially if you have children, you will need a safety plan. Telling them you will leave them is not always the smartest move. Seek professional advice.

Healing is essential when you go through such a breakup; you question where it went wrong, where you went wrong, whether that person ever loved you, and whether it was all fake. I drive myself insane by asking questions because I cannot get closure. I have no doubt I have driven my friends and family to boredom or complete frustration as I have been hurt and humiliated again and again. I do not hate anyone or anything that has happened in my life.

It is very lonely at times; it is hard when you are the only single person in that room at christenings and weddings. But let me tell you a little secret: most of these married couples are in abusive relationships, and you should hold your head up high for getting out.

There are many casualties with domestic abuse, and it is not one quick fix to taking someone out of the situation. Without the consistency of unconditional love from my family, this could have ended very differently. Some acquaintances and friends have come and gone. I haven't spoken about my friends, but I left many of them as part of my journey. I had to leave my friend initially and pull away from others for over ten years. Friends that I have known since having Roma and Jake know very little, and I know a couple who would be frustrated at me for not telling them so they could help me. You know who you are. I have apologised to your face for leaving some of you, but please forgive me for walking away.

Normal to me is being at home with my children and family. I now have grandchildren whom I absolutely adore. Many years ago, I had a cam recorder, which I used nearly every day and for my children's special events. Now, we have mobile phones and iPads with this facility on them, so it's easier. As a birthday present to my Mum, I paid for the tapes to become discs so we could watch them occasionally. These times were my happiest; we had nothing but each other. I had just bought my house, started a new job and made some very special friends. My friends have remained with me through good and bad times, providing support and kindness to me and my family. We watch these recordings regularly. Often, the children remarked that the house was not often tidy, with the number of toys scattered around every room and the garden. Still, they were always laughing and joking around.

I have studied and have now established myself into a career. I am now a trainer of domestic abuse. To support others to get through it, you must undertake therapy to gain knowledge of your resilience and strengths and to work on your vulnerabilities. Most perpetrators have been the victim of some kind of abuse, and we need to promote that they do something about it. Don't live in silence; be brave and talk to someone if you are suffering. When delivering training, people will share a story asking for support and advice; sometimes, it will be for someone else, or indeed, it will be for themselves. We need more perpetrator programmes and for survivors to have an insight into what makes them vulnerable to this type of behaviour. Without this experience, I probably would not have gone so far, but I had to show my children that if you work hard and never give up, you will always bounce back after disappointment.

Roma has a lovely boyfriend and lots of friends. Jake is my handsome boy who is not ready for a relationship but wants to become independent within the next couple of years. Georgina will be a homeowner one day with Joe; they both work hard, and Mable, Martha and Callum do not wish for anything. So, life is busy; everyone is doing their own thing.

So, what is normal? What is fucked up? I have been mocked for not having anyone or no one reliable in the past. I have been mocked for not having the wisdom to identify dangerous traits which others can clearly see. I have been let down and betrayed by people I thought I could trust at work, at home, in friendship circles, and even acquaintances who assume I am a party girl and have a string of boyfriends. I have been used and exploited sexually.

Many people ask, 'Why would you put up with it? I would never put up with a man doing that to me, let alone two.' I hope they change their views after reading this book. As a survivor, we are not weak; any survivor of abuse is strong and does not need to be judged but supported by others.

I am not an angel; I have not lived like a nun. I have also maintained my dignity. Other than a few monsters, I have met some lovely men I have not mentioned who have treated me like a goddess and tried to make a go at relationships. Why did it not work? Sometimes, it's just too good to be true. A victim of domestic abuse can also become the self-saboteur of any future happiness, returning to the attention of a narcissist. I was not ready, and I am sorry for how I treated you.

Unfortunately, at times, I have had a few moments where I have been vulnerable; my daughter thinks I fall for men too quick; she hasn't a clue, really. I have used and abused men just as much as they have used me. When we broke up over an insignificant issue, I was bad at times and dated a new man a week later. The insignificant others I can't be bothered to describe in this book always message me later, wanting a reconciliation; sometimes I have, but mainly not. Fuck them they had their chance.

I have always held it together. COVID-19 brought it back, taunting me in my dreams and suppressed feelings and images lost many years ago. Also, my recent experience with Simon has affected my pride and self-confidence and broken my heart.

After reading this, I advise you to know who you are and reflect on what is good and where relationships have gone wrong. You will love again and find that soulmate where it does not matter about the past. It is the future where either you step alone or hold their hand. It is okay to be single, and you do not have to put up with abuse. Finally, remember that your children listen when you think they are in another room; they feel the tension even inside the womb. Be wise when choosing who you love and who fits that gap. You will be happy again.

I continue to suffer the nightmares, but I am no longer living or existing in this kind of relationship anymore. I am currently dating after months, as I say, hibernation. When I see a red flag, I reflect to see if I am overthinking or letting them go. I have been back on that floor but managed to get up again.

Julia xxx